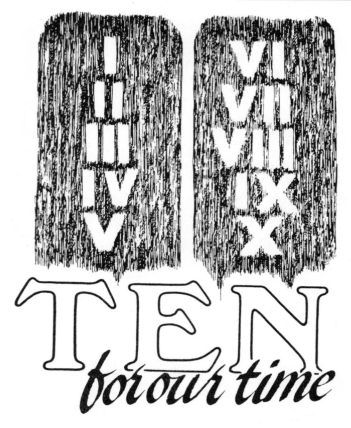

TEN *for our time*

A NEW LOOK AT THE TEN COMMANDMENTS

LOWELL O. ERDAHL

C.S.S. Publishing Company, Inc.
Lima, Ohio

Other books by Lowell O. Erdahl:

Be Good to Each Other: An Open Letter on Marriage
(co-authored with Carol Erdahl)

Pro Life/Pro Peace: Life Affirming Alternatives to Abortion, War, Mercy killing and the Death Penalty

6804 / ISBN 0-89536-786-6   PRINTED IN U.S.A.

Dedication
To the members and friends of University Lutheran Church of Hope who were people of encouragement during our decade together.

In Appreciation

I am grateful to Professor Daniel Simundson and Paul Sponheim of Luther Northwestern Theological Seminary, Pastors Orville Olson, Myrwood Bagne, and Ted Vinger, for their suggestions and encouragement; to Mary Knutson and Doris Nelson, who typed early drafts; and to Kathy Malchow, who prepared the final manuscript.

Table of Contents

Preface

Ten For Our Time is a readable, helpful look at the Ten Commandments. As Bishop Erdahl suggests, it is neither sermons nor scholarly exegesis, but it could be useful for the preacher and it shows familiarity with the latter. These are insightful and thought provoking reflections on the meaning and implications of these ancient standards of conduct for our own day. The original sense of the commandments for ancient Israel is important, but, for Erdahl, that does not exhaust their significance for us. He often makes the specific point that we Christians are to read them in the light of Jesus' life and teachings.

Erdahl has a positive approach to the commandments. He sees them as a gift from God, for our benefit. They are not a ladder by which we can climb to God. Rather, they are given to a people already delivered and loved. That positive approach to the commandments pervades the whole book. Readers will not feel that they are being scolded and burdened with an endless list of obligations and duties.

The book is well written, clear, with good illustrations and anecdotes (many drawn from the author's personal and pastoral experience) that connect to our everyday life.

Erdahl presents sensible, balanced discussions on each commandment. There is lots of good common sense. He is open to other points of view, but is direct in letting us know what is his own position, even on some of the thornier ethical questions of our day — such as abortion, capital punishment, euthanasia, suicide, war, divorce, homsexuality, and our use of the world's resources. One may disagree with his conclusions on some of these issues but must respect the consistent and careful way in which he presents his views.

Daniel J. Simundson
Professor of Old Testament
Luther Northwestern Theological Seminary
Saint Paul, Minnesota

Introduction

"Most of us haven't heard much about the Ten Commandments since we were confirmed. Therefore, I think you should preach some sermons on the Ten Commandments." This suggestion from Roger Asp, a member of University Lutheran Church of Hope in Minneapolis where I was then pastor, prompted a sermon series on the Ten Commandments.

Those sermons have been revised and reworked into the chapters contained in this book. They are no longer sermons, nor are they scholarly exegetical commentary on the Ten Commandments. They are reflections that seek to share some of the message and meaning of these "Ten for Our Time."

I believe the Ten Commandments speak to us at this time as they have spoken to others in every previous generation and that they are gifts from God with love. The Ten Commandments are given to bless us. They are ten gifts for our good.

I also believe the commandments' meaning for us is larger than the understanding of those who first received them. Few Christians, for example, now understand "You shall not commit adultery" to require a wife's faithfulness to her husband, while allowing him to have additional wives and concubines. We understand all of Scripture, including the Ten Commandments, in the context of Christ and are therefore bold, as was Luther, in adding his positive interpretations, to proclaim meanings larger than those understood by Moses and the people of Israel more than 3,000 years ago.

The Ten Commandments are as timely as they are timeless. They relate to contemporary, and sometimes controversial, issues such as abortion and contraception, to which the biblical writers refer incidentally if at all. Since we have no direct "Word from the Lord" about such matters, our comments must be in the nature of reasoned reflections rather than dogmatic declarations. Some will likely take issue with some of my specific understanding of what the commandments now mean for us, but if these reflections serve to stimulate thought and promote discussion, I will be grateful.

A Numbers Game

We have been taught that there are ten commandments recorded in Exodus twenty and Deuteronomy five, but neither of these texts tells us how to number them. As you read them now, not from the abbreviated version you may remember from the catechism, but from the text of the Revised Standard Version of Exodus 20:1-17, imagine you have never seen them before, and then decide where you would put the numbers.

And God spoke all these words, saying, "I am the LORD your God, who brought you out of the land of Egypt, out of the house of bondage.

"You shall have no other gods before me.

"You shall not make for yourself a graven image, or any likeness of anything that is in the heaven above, that is in the earth beneath, or that is in the water under the earth; you shall not bow down to them or serve them; for I the LORD your God am a jealous God, visiting the iniquity of the fathers upon the children to the third and the fourth generation of those who hate me, but showing steadfast love to thousands of those who love me and keep my commandments.

"You shall not take the name of the LORD your God in vain; for the LORD will not hold him guiltless who takes his name in vain.

"Remember the sabbath day, to keep it holy. Six days you shall labor, and do all your work; but the seventh day is the sabbath to the LORD your God; in it you shall not do any work, you, or your son, or your daughter, your manservant, or your maidservant, or your cattle, or the sojourner who is within your gates; for in six days the LORD made heaven and earth, the sea, and all that is in them, and rested the seventh day; therefore the LORD blessed the

sabbath day and hallowed it.

"Honor your father and your mother, that your days may be long in the land which the LORD your God gives you.

"You shall not kill.

"You shall not commit adultery.

"You shall not steal.

"You shall not bear false witness against your neighbor.

"You shall not covet your neighbor's house; you shall not covet your neighbor's wife, or his manservant, or his maidservant, or his ox, or his ass, or anything that is your neighbor's."

Where did you put the numbers? Those of us who learned the Ten Commandments from Luther's Small Catechism may habitually number them as he did following the practice of the Roman Catholic Church. The Roman Catholics combined the verses about having "No other gods before me," and "You shall not make for yourself a graven image . . ." into one commandment and then, so as to come out with ten rather than only nine commandments, they divided verse seventeen which deals with coveting, into two commandments.

If we were unfamiliar with the Roman Catholic/Lutheran way of numbering the commandments, I doubt we would number them that way. From a study of the content of the commandments in the biblical text, we would more likely number them as do most Protestants and Greek Orthodox Christians: First, "You shall have no other gods before me"; second, "You shall not make for yourselves a graven image or any likeness . . ."; third, "You shall not take the name of the LORD your God in vain"; etc., through the rest of the commandments concluding with only one commandment on coveting.

It is significant to note that there is yet a third way of numbering the commandments, which is that of the Jewish community who, of course, received them in the first place. They understand the introductory statement in Exodus 20:2 "I am the LORD your God who brought you out of the land of Egypt, out of the house of bondage'' to be the first commandment. There are at least two reasons why such numbering seems strange to us. In the first place, this statement doesn't even sound like a commandment. It is a declaration that doesn't command us to do anything. But, as Jewish teachers are quick to point out, it does clearly imply that we are to do something — namely to live in remembrance of the fact that the Lord is our God and that we are his delivered people. Therefore, in effect, the Jewish community puts the word "remember" in front of the declaration in verse two and it then becomes the first and most basic of all the commandments — "Remember, I am the LORD your God who brought you out of the land of Egypt, out of the house of bondage."

The other reason for Christians not regarding verse two as the first commandment is that most of us are Gentiles whose ancestors were never freed from slavery in Egypt. Yet, when we remember the story of the people of Israel is also our story, and the book of the Old Covenant is also our book, and realize, that in Christ we are the new Israel, it becomes clear that, in a profound and significant sense, this verse *does* apply to us. In Christ we also are a delivered people. In Christ we have been brought out of slavery to sin and death, out of that house of bondage into the glorious liberty of the children of God. Therefore, we rightly relate verse two to ourselves and hear it saying: "Remember, I am the LORD your God who brought you out of slavery to sin, out of the house of bondage to fear and death, and into new life in Christ."

How we number the commandments is not a matter of ultimate significance. Their content is the same regardless of where we put the numbers. But we miss something important by neglecting verse two. Recalling the Jewish first commandment helps us to remember these commandments are not given as a ladder by which we climb to God. They are given to people who are already loved, already God's people, already delivered and set free from the house of bondage. Remembering that verse helps us to keep all the commandments in the context of the grace and mercy of the saving God we know in Jesus Christ our Lord. However we number them, all of the commandments are grounded in God's gracious deliverance.

There is an implied "therefore" which stands at the end of verse two and, in effect, before each of the specific commandments. That "therefore" is in fact stated in Scripture:

> *"And because he loved your fathers and chose their descendents after them, and brought you out of Egypt with his own presence, by his great power . . . know therefore this day, and lay it to your heart, that the LORD is God in heaven above and on earth beneath; there is no other. Therefore you shall keep his statutes and his commandments, which I command you this day, that it may go well with you, and with your children after you, that you may prolong your days in the land which the LORD your God gives you forever."*
> *(Deuteronomy 4:37, 39, 40; emphasis added)*

Pondering this statement reminds us of a much later word which gives us the context of all Christian living: "Beloved, if God so loved us, we also ought to love one another . . . We love, because he first loved us." (1 John 4:11, 19)

Although I have reservations about doing so, I will abide by my own heritage and, in these chapters, follow the Lutheran/Roman Catholic numbering of the commandments. I will also follow the practice of most catechetical texts within this tradition by combining the presentation of the ninth and tenth commandments into a single chapter on coveting. A concluding chapter, "Love: The First and Final Word," seeks to sum up the meaning of all the commandments in the context of Christ.

Concluding each chapter are questions and suggestions for reflection and discussion. These are intended to stimulate personal reflection and group conversation. They are designed for use by congregational forums and by teenagers and adults participating in a study series on the Ten Commandments. This book, and the questions concluding each chapter, can also be used as a resource for Confirmation instruction concerning the Ten Commandments.

Questions and Suggestions For Reflection and Discussion

The suggestions and questions in this section are intended for use in an introductory session at the beginning of a study series on the Ten Commandments. With only brief interpretation, all of the questions can be discussed prior to reading the Introduction in the book.

1. Read both accounts of the Ten Commandments — in Exodus 20:1-17 and Deuteronomy 5:6-21. What are your first impressions? How are the accounts similar? How are they different?

2. Why did God give us the Ten Commandments?

3. Do you agree that the Ten Commandments mean more for us than for those who first received them? Why? Why not?

4. Was Martin Luther justified, in his catechism, in giving each of the commandments a positive as well as negative meaning? Why? Why not?

5. Are we justified in relating the Ten Commandments to matters such as abortion and contraception, to which they do not refer directly? Why? Why not?

6. Imagine you have never heard of the Ten Commandments; then turn again to the accounts in Exodus 20 and Deuteronomy 5 and number them as seems most fitting to the biblical text. Where did you put the numbers? Why?

7. The Introduction refers to Roman Catholic/Lutheran, general Protestant, and Jewish ways of numbering the Ten Commandments. Which seems most appropriate to you? Why? Which least appropriate? Why?

8. What difference does the numbering make to our understanding of the Ten Commandments?

9. What is the significance of Exodus 20:2 and Deuteronomy 5:6? In what sense do these declarations apply to us?

10. What is the difference between regarding the Ten Commandments, on the one hand, as a ladder by which we climb to God or, on the other hand, as gifts for the good of an already delivered people?

11. What is the significance of the "therefores" in Deuteronomy 4:39 and 40? And of the "therefore" not stated, but which is clearly implied, between Deuteronomy 5:6 and 5:7?

12. What do 1 John 4:11 and 19 teach us concerning a right understanding of the Ten Commandments?

Chapter 1

Let God Be God

"Let God be God." These words give Philip Watson's summary of Martin Luther's witness to the world. They also give the gist of the meaning of the First Commandment: "You shall have no other gods before me." (Exodus 20:3; Deuteronomy 5:7)

The wording of the First Commandment, especially when understood in light of Luther's statement that this means "we should fear, love and trust in God above anything else" may convey a subtle but dangerous misconception. These statements may be heard to say that it is all right to have other gods provided they are not trusted or worshiped "before" or "above" the one true God.

Our Greater Danger

Our greater danger is not a blatant idolatry, which rejects the true God, but a more subtle polytheism which seeks to trust and worship several "gods" at the same time. When Aaron yielded to the people's pressure and made the golden calf, he did not intend it to replace the true God of Israel. Having built an altar before the golden calf, "Aaron made proclamation and said 'tomorrow shall be a feast to the LORD.' " (Exodus 32:5) Today they would worship the golden calf; tomorrow they would worship "the LORD" — that is "Yahweh," the true God of Israel.

Is something similar true for us? Do we, all week long, trust and worship false gods of personal and corporate privilege and power and then, on Sunday, come to church to confess and worship the true God? When accused of such idolatry, we may retreat to the letter of the commandment and of Luther's meaning and excuse ourselves by saying that, in our heart of hearts, we do not put anything "before" or "above" the one true God. It is, therefore, well to take a closer look at this commandment and its context. When we do, we note two things of vital importance. First, the Hebrew word translated "before" can also be translated "besides," so Exodus 20:3 and Deuteronomy 5:7 can also read "You shall have no other gods besides me." Secondly, we note that the verses immediately following this statement, in both Exodus and Deuteronomy, (which are understood by many to be the second commandment) forbid the worship of any false gods whatsoever and declare "I the Lord your God am a jealous God." (Exodus 20:5; Deuteronomy 5:9) This reminds us of statements such as, "You shall worship no other god, for the LORD whose name is Jealous is a jealous God." (Exodus 34:14) We are, therefore, not just to refrain from having any other gods "before" or "above" God. We are to have "no other god" period! That means no god above, or beside, or even below the one true God.

Our Non-Jealous "gods"

Only the one true God has a right to be jealous. He is, as Luther liked to say, "The only God there is." The false gods who tempt our trust and worship are not jealous gods. They do not demand our total allegiance and exclusive loyalty, but only our daily obedience and periodic service. They are glad to have us go to church on Sunday, to confess our faith, sing our hymns, and say our prayers. They, in fact, affirm and defend our worship and our prayers. The god of wealth, for example, is glad to have us go to church and to thank God for our prosperity. The god of national pride and power is glad to have us worship our true God, even in the White House, and may even advocate required prayers in the public schools. These are not jealous gods. When we come to our dying hour they are willing to be abandoned altogether and will let us go with gratitude for all we have done to obey and serve them. Then they will let God be "all in all" and, until then, ask only our temporal trust and weekly allegiance.

To illustrate the attitude of these non-jealous gods, I recall a conversation with a married woman who confessed to being involved in an affair with a married man. I inquired concerning the effect of this affair upon her marriage and upon his. She replied that their marriages were going on as well, if not better, than usual. When I asked how her new lover felt about this and how she felt about

about his continued relationship with his wife, she sensed, correctly, I was naive concerning the ground rules of extramarital affairs, and went on to explain that people in such involvements do not expect sexual faithfulness of each other. They realize their lovers will continue to have sexual relations with their spouses, and may even hope they will do so more than ever so there will be no grounds for suspicion of the affair.

In a similar way, our false gods ask our love and affection but do not demand our faithfulness. In this case, their lack of jealousy is not a virtue, but is part of the seductivity that tempts us to love and serve them, even as we continue to worship the one true God. When we yield to their seductive power we are not only guilty of idolatry but actually of polytheism — the worship of many gods. One of these may be the true God. All others are false gods and idols.

Contemporary Idols

None of us, when sane and sober, can be seduced into dancing around a golden calf. If someone were to suggest, "Here is a golden calf for you to worship,' we would likely consider it a joke and respond with scorn or laughter. The idols who tempt our worship are far more subtle and deceptive than that. Some of these idols are private gods of personal prestige and power. We are all tempted to worship the paltry little triune god "Me, Myself and I" Excessive trust in, and adoration of, an idolatrous "self" is not far from any one of us, nor is idolatrous trust in money and property and the worship of popularity and success.

Beyond these private gods, there are the corporate "deities" of the state and nation in which we live. One among these is the "god" of the nation itself. We rightly thank God for our country, and believe in proper patriotism. Nationalism has its place. But, as we look at the history of nations, we see how easy it is for proper patriotism and nationalism to become idolatrous jingoism. When we are willing to sacrifice our own children and the children of other nations, to keep our nation number one, supreme and sovereign above all others, we have gone beyond legitimate nationalism. To say "I will obey my country no matter what it asks me to do," is not proper patriotism, but sinful idolatry. As American Christians, our supreme allegiance must always be to Jesus Christ and not to Uncle Sam.

Robert Jay Lifton, the Yale psychiatrist, points to another

deceptive idol of our time which he calls "the nuclear deity." We are less enamored of nuclear power than we were a few years ago, when it seemed to promise endless energy and prosperity, but we still look to "the nuclear deity" of atomic weaponry to guarantee our security and safety. Most of us believe in the necessity of responsible and limited police power in a sinful world, but there is great difference between reliance upon responsible and limited police power and idolatrous dependence upon doomsday weapons that threaten to destroy all they are intended to defend.

The god of material wealth is corporate as well as personal. Although we are only about six percent of the world's population, we consume twenty-five to thirty percent of some of the world's resources. We even claim, because we consume so much, it is our right to continue to do so. We declare that the oil beneath distant deserts belongs to us and that we will go to war to keep it. Have we become so attached to our mode of transportation that we will, in effect, kill for our cars? If so, we may also be guilty of worshiping an automotive deity.

Think, too, of how we can make a false god of American ingenuity and inventiveness. When someone speaks of the limits of growth and of declining resources — when we hear of "entropy" and how the world's resources are being changed from the useable to the useless — the response is often, "Don't worry about it. We can solve every problem. Our science and technology will save us." It's great to be confident and hopeful, but is not such trust, saying "We can do anything and save ourselves from every problem," a form of idolatry of technology that will finally let us down?

Note part of the explanation of the First Commandment in Luther's *Large Catechism*:

> *What is it to have a god or what is God? A God is that to which we look for all good and where we resort for help in every time of need. To have a God is simply to trust and believe in one with our whole heart. As I have often said, the confidence and faith of the heart make both God and an idol. If your faith and confidence are right, then likewise your God is the true God. On the other hand, if your confidence is false, if it is wrong, then you have not a true God . . . Whatever our heart clings to and confides in, that is really your God.*

To whom do we turn in time of need? In what, or in whom, do we trust with the central confidence of our hearts? In commandment and in Christ, Scripture proclaims the one right answer to such questions, "Let God be God!" All other gods are really no gods at all. If our central trust is in ourselves, in our money, in the power of wealth or nation, or in anything other than God, we have, by that trust, created an idol and are living a false and foolish faith.

Many of our idols are not evil in themselves; they may even be good, but they are not God. We were created good, but we are not gods; money is good, but it is not God. There is much good about America, but our government is not God. We ought to be anxious when we trust good things as God for then they are idols that will finally fail us. Such misplaced confidence needs to be broken and the sooner the better for us. There is truth in an old rabbinic saying, "It is better to have no god than the wrong god." Our greater danger is not atheism but idolatry. It is better for us to know the despair of having nothing in which to trust, than to place our trust in a false god that is no God at all.

Opportunity in Extremity

When the foundations of such false faith tremble and we are shaken to recognize the weakness of the false gods in which we are trusting, there is still hope for us. It is then true that "Our extremities are God's opportunities." In our anxiety, we hear again the witness of Scripture speaking personally to each of us, "I am the Lord your God. I have delivered you. You are mine. I have brought you out of the house of bondage, you shall have no other gods before me or beside me."

In his beautiful book *Kept Moments,* Gerhard Frost asks, "Prayer? What is it but letting God be God, letting him love you in your being and in your becoming?"[1] Even as we are seduced and entangled in a dozen adulterous idolatries, the God and Father of our Lord Jesus Christ, the God of mercy and the God of might, the God of awesome power and tender love, the only God there is, calls us, in Christ, out of our idolatry into renewed confidence and trust, into new surrender that lets God be God for us. In Christ, God says to each of us, "Rest in my love and power. Trust me in joy and in sorrow. Give me alone the central confidence, loyalty and allegiance of your heart." When we yield to that invitation, we let God be God by letting him love us in our being and in our becoming.

ENDNOTES

[1]Gerhard E. Frost, *Kept Moments.* Minneapolis, MN: Winston Press, 1982, p. 64.

Questions and Suggestions for Reflection and Discussion

1. Do you agree that our greater danger is not "blatant idolatry" but "subtle polytheism"? Why? Why not?

2. What is the significance of the footnote to both Exodus 20:3 and Deuteronomy 5:7, in the Revised Standard Version, which states that "before" can also be translated "besides"?

3. In what ways do we trust and worship false gods before, besides, or even below the one true God?

4. Do you agree that while the one true God is jealous, the false gods are not? Why might this be true?

5. What do our false gods expect of us? What does the one true God expect?

6. What are our most common false gods?

7. When do we make a god of self? Of wealth? Of nation? Of anything?

8. Do you agree most false gods are not bad things, but good things in God's place? Why? Why not?

9. How do you understand Robert Jay Lifton's reference to "the nuclear deity"? In what way does this witness to a false god?

10. In what ways do we idolize science and technology? What is wrong with having such a false god?

11. Do you agree "It is better to have no God than the wrong God"? Why? Why not?

12. What can we do to keep the first commandment and to help each other keep it? What sins does this commandment prompt us to confess?

13. What amendment of life does this commandment challenge us to make?

14. Do you agree "Let God be God" sums up the meaning of the First Commandment? Why? Why not?

Chapter 2

Hallowed Be Thy Name

Moses taught the people of Israel, "You shall not take the name of the LORD your God in vain, for the LORD will not hold him guiltless who takes his name in vain." (Exodus 20:7 and Deuteronomy 5:11) Jesus taught his disciples to pray, "Our Father who art in heaven, hallowed be thy name." (Matthew 6:9)

Most of us understand the second commandment as a prohibition against cursing and swearing. It *is* that, but that is not the whole of it. The second commandment, like the first petition of the Lord's Prayer, relates not just to the *names* we use for God, but to the *name* of God — "Hallowed be thy *name*. You shall not take the *name* of the LORD Your God in vain." (Emphasis added) An old explanation of Luther's Small Catechism asked the question, "What is meant by God's name?" and gave this answer: "God's name means God himself revealed in his word and works.

The prohibition in the second commandment is not just against cursing and swearing, but against lives of irreverence — lives lived without a sense of awe and holy respect for the presence of God. When we pray in the first petition, "Hallowed be thy name," we are not just praying for reverent speech, but for lives of respect and reverence toward God. Moses and Jesus call us to live with a sense of the sacred and holy presence of God.

Capacity for Reverence

When understood in this way, the second commandment

and the first petition of the Lord's Prayer speak to one of the most significant and unique capacities God has given to us as human beings — the capacity for reverence. Does the rest of the animal kingdom have this capacity? Does the cow in the pasture, or the hog in the trough have capacity for reverence? In the beautiful old translation of "O Day Full of Grace," we sang "the birds in the morning sing God's praise." That may be true but, as far as we know, the birds do not bow in conscious reverence and awe before the holy presence of God. The creatures of the animal kingdom seem to be without the capacity for either personal sin or conscious reverence, but these are certainly human capacities.

Reverence is the thought and emotion we experience in the presence of that which is far greater than ourselves. We may be moved to reverence by the presence of great beauty and great love. We are moved to awe and adoration as we ponder the greatness and goodness of God. Reverence is akin to terror. It rightly contains aspects of holy fear. Years ago, at a national church convention, there was a debate over whether Luther's introduction to the meaning of each of the commandments in the Small Catechism should be translated, "We should fear and love God," or, "We should reverence and love God." Since the debaters made a good case for each translation, it is well to remember both versions. We are to reverence and fear God. We rightly tremble with awe and wonder before his holy presence.

Naming the Name

Reverencing the holiness of God as we honor God's *name* leads to respectful use of the *names* of God. In his meaning of the second commandment, Luther stresses that we are not to use God's name "superstitiously or use it to curse, swear, lie or deceive" but we are to call upon God in every time of need and to worship him with "prayer, praise and thanksgiving." As we respect and reverence God's holy presence with us, we certainly will not spitefully use God's names to curse, swear, or blaspheme, nor will we wish to use the names of God and Jesus in profanity or casual disrespect.

In the Sermon on the Mount, Jesus says, "Do not swear

at all, either by heaven, for it is the throne of God, or by the earth, for it is his footstool . . . Let what you say be simply 'Yes' or 'No'. Anything more than this comes from evil.'' (Matthew 5:34, 35, 37) We are to speak the truth plainly and clearly, with all expletives deleted, and are never to use God's name in oaths, to cover our lies and half truths. For us Christians, the irreverent use of God's name is both sinful and superfluous. It is both heedless of God and needless to our conversation.

Matters of Mind and Heart

As with the name of God, our use of the names of God is a matter of mind and heart, as well as talk. God "hears" the attitudes of our hearts, as well as the words we speak.

Luther reminds us that the curses of the blasphemers may sound more pleasing to the ears of God than some of the prayers of the pious. He may have been thinking of prayers like that of the proud, self-righteous Pharisee who thanked God he was so much better than everyone else. (See Luke 18:9-14.) Luther says that kind of praying is profane. Our pride and pretense, our self-righteous and judgmental attitudes — all these are profanities of the heart.

Verbal expression of honest anger may be less profane than the proud and spiteful sweetness we sometimes use to cover our hostility, and it may also be healthier for us and for others with whom we live. This may be what Paul Tournier, who has written so insightfully of our life in Christ, means when he says "Neurotics are people who can't say 'damn it'." In quoting that statement I am not advocating profanity, but honesty. Just as we are not to take God's name in vain, so also we are not to dishonestly bottle up our anger or wrap our resentments in a cloak of pious pretense that may sicken ourselves and our relationships with others.

Psalm 4:4 says, "Be angry but sin not." Ephesians 4:26 says, "Be angry but do not sin." We, therefore, seek ways of honestly expressing our anger, without either defaming or degrading the name of God or making ourselves and others sick by our lack of sincerity. Those of us who are shocked to even *think* swear words, let alone to ever *say* them, are not, thereby, innocent of breaking this commandment. Others who may be more expressive are not necessarily more profane. They may only be more honest. God, who sees our hearts, is alone the judge of us all.

As we confront this commandment, we are again driven back to the grace and mercy of God in Jesus Christ. With word and attitude, we have all broken this commandment. We have, too often, been like the cow in the pasture and the hog in the trough. We have been less than human in living lives without awe and wonder before God's holy presence. Whether our sins are of word or attitude, God does not hold those guiltless who take his name in vain. We must give account of our words and of our attitudes. As we sense our guilt, we thank God again for his great grace and mercy in Christ our Lord.

Great Sin but Greater Grace

As a striking, even shocking, illustration of dependence upon mercy, in relation to sin against this commandment, I recall an intense encounter with a parishioner who was outraged by the unexpected death of his friend. When he got word of that death, he was not moved to say, with Job, "The LORD gave and the LORD has taken away; blessed be the name of the LORD." (Job 1:21) He was moved to anger and rage, like that of which Dylan Thomas speaks in a poem at the death of his father: "Do not go gentle into that good night, rage, rage, against the dying of the light." In confession, my parishioner told that, in his rage, he cried, "God damn it!" If the "it" in that expression refers to death, there may be a biblical basis for its use as a prayer rather than profanity. The Apocalypse declares, "Then Death and Hades were thrown into the lake of fire" (Revelation 20:14) and Paul states, "The last enemy to be destroyed is death." (1 Corinthians 15:26) These verses remind us that the God of life will, at the end, damn death to destruction. But when my parishioner confessed his use of such language, he acknowledged it to be a sin, and then made a statement I have never forgotten. "My God," he said, "is too big to worry about times when I get angry and say 'God damn it'."

I do not recommend the use of such language, even in situations of grief and anger. But I do advocate trust in that kind of great God — the kind of God who is great enough in holiness to move us again and again to bow in reverence before him — the kind of God who is great enough in mercy to assure us that, though we sin, he still loves and forgives and cares for us. Peter, like my parishioner, had that kind of God. Peter denied Jesus with a curse and yet Christ welcomed him again and he was forgiven and commissioned to witness to that great mercy. This is the great God we know in Christ and his cross and resurrection. This is the great God who, in Christ, invites us to come to the sacrament of his broken body and shed blood to receive again and again the assurance that, in spite of all our irreverence — the irreverence of our hearts and of our lips — in spite of all the sins that are in us — sins God knows better than we know ourselves — in spite of it all, God still loves us. In Christ we are still forgiven. In Christ, we are still God's children, created and redeemed to live in reverence before God's holy presence, and then to use God's holy names to worship God with prayer, praise, and thanksgiving.

Questions and Suggestions for
Reflection and Discussion

1. What is meant by God's "name"?

2. What is the difference between God's "name" and God's "names"?

3. How do we take God's "name" in vain? How do we keep God's "name" holy?

4. Do you agree that every human being has a capacity for reverence? If so, how do we exercise this capacity?

5. What is the difference between "fearing" God and "reverencing" God? Are we to do both? Why? Why not?

6. How do we misuse the names of God? How do we rightly honor and use God's names?

7. What prompts people to curse and swear? What is wrong with such people on the inside?

8. How do we break this commandment without using any words? In what ways can our prayers, like those of the Pharisee, be profane?

9. Do you agree with Paul Tournier that "neurotics are people who can't say 'damn it'"? What does this imply concerning the healthy and holy expression of negative feelings?

10. In relation to Ephesians 4:26, how can we express our anger without sinning?

11. What does it mean to pray "in Jesus' name"?

12. In what ways does confrontation with this commandment drive us to Christ? What sins does it prompt us to confess? What do we receive from Christ?

13. What amendment of life does this commandment challenge us to make?

14. What can we do to keep, and to help each other keep, this commandment?

Chapter 3

A Day To Remember

"Remember the sabbath day to keep it holy." One day of rest and worship — a day for special caring — this "sabbath day" is God's gift for our good.

Scripture witnesses to several meanings of the Sabbath, and of the Lord's day. Note first these words from the Exodus account of the Ten Commandments.

> *Remember the sabbath day, to keep it holy. Six days you shall labor, and do all your work; but the seventh day is a sabbath to the LORD your God; in it you shall not do any work, you, or your son, or your daughter, your manservant, or your maidservant, or your cattle, or the sojourner who is within your gates; for in six days the LORD made heaven and earth, the sea, and all that is in them, and rested the seventh day; therefore the LORD blessed the sabbath day and hallowed it. (Exodus 20:8-11)*

As God Rested

In this text, Sabbath observance is grounded in creation and in the story of God's own resting. "In six days the LORD made the heaven and the earth, the sea, and all that is in them, and rested the seventh day; *therefore* the LORD blessed the sabbath day and hallowed it" (emphasis added). We are created in the image of a working and resting God. As God works, we are to work. As God rested, we are to rest. Even the cattle and other beasts of burden (see Deuteronomy 5:14) are to rest.

These verses remind us that the necessity for rest is built into God's design of creation. It is wise, as well as moral, to keep this commandment. A day of rest is God's blessing to help us be the persons we are designed to be, and to live the lives we are created to live. It is truly one of God's gifts for our good.

This commandment speaks directly to workaholics who have difficulty taking time for rest and refreshment. "The best day in my life," said one workaholic, "was the day I resigned from being Chairman of the Board of the universe." If God could take time to rest, so can we. Such times of rest are not wasted. They are a vital necessity for our renewal and more responsible living.

We pastors may be among the greatest sinners against this commandment, and not just because some of our responsibilities fall on Sunday. We easily get so caught up in the activities and responsibilities of parish life, we neglect to set time apart for rest, refreshment, and renewal. Such renewal is essential, not only for our personal health, but also for meaningful ministry over extended time. We need to remember the congregation is in God's hands and not ours alone, and that God gives each of us enough time to do what he wants us to do, even though it may seem less than what is needed for what we ourselves, or our congregations, expect us to do. We all have limits and need to listen to our bodies, minds, and spirits as they call for rest and refreshment. Those who would give must take time to receive or, soon, they will have nothing to give. To sin against this commandment is not just to go against a religious rule — it is to go against our own creation and against the will of our creator. To keep this commandment is to live in harmony with our design and to be faithful to the image of our creator.

Remember Your Savior

When we compare the Exodus and Deuteronomy accounts of the Third Commandment, we discover that Deuteronomy gives a different reason for observing the Sabbath. Note how the statements are essentially identical except for the last sentence.

Observe the sabbath day, to keep it holy, as the LORD your God commanded you. Six days you shall labor, and do all your work; but the seventh day is a sabbath to the LORD your God; in it you shall not do any work, you, or your son, or your daughter, or your manservant, or your maidservant, or your ox, or your ass, or any of your cattle, or the sojourner who is within your gates, that your manservant and your maidservant may rest as well as you. You shall remember that you were a servant in the land of Egypt, and the LORD your God brought you out thence with a mighty hand and an outstretched arm; therefore *the LORD your God commanded you to keep the sabbath day." (Deuteronomy 5:12-15; emphasis added)*

Exodus relates Sabbath remembrance to creation and to God's own resting. But in Deuteronomy the reason is not in creation but in salvation — in God's mighty deliverance of his people. Note that last verse again. It doesn't say anything about God's resting. It calls for remembrance of the time of slavery in Egypt and of God's great deliverance. Then it says "therefore" — "therefore the LORD your God commanded you to keep the sabbath day." (Deuteronomy 5:15) Here the basis of the Sabbath observance is not in God's rest, but in God's rescue. The Sabbath is for remembrance of being a saved and delivered people. It is given for the remembrance and worship of God who was, and still is, our Savior.

The people of Israel see God's deliverance from their bondage in Egypt as the central saving event in their history. Among Jewish people that deliverance is remembered not only in the annual observance of the Passover, but also in the weekly observance of the Sabbath. The Sabbath stands as a continual sign of, and witness to, God's deliverance.

As people of the New Israel, who have sometimes been described as "honorary Jews," we join in celebrating that deliverance. But, for us, the center of salvation is not in the Exodus, but in the Christ and his cross and resurrection. It is therefore not surprising the early Christians gradually shifted their Sabbath observance from the seventh day of the week, the day of the remembrance of the Exodus, to Sunday, the day of remembrance of the resurrection. Every Sunday was a celebration of Easter, and they soon began to call it, "The Lord's Day." (Revelation 1:10)

The Sabbath for Jews, and the Lord's Day for Christians, are not just days for rest. They are days for remembrance of our salvation. Sunday is a day for worshipful remembrance of God's deliverance in Christ our Lord, who has set us free, not just from slavery in a foreign land, but from bondage to sin and death. The first commandment says, in effect, "Let God be God." The second commandment calls for reverence to honor God's presence. The third commandment calls us to let that reverence break forth in worshipful praise and thanksgiving. As we confess Christ as Lord and Savior, it is right and good for us to take time to give God thanks and praise.

When we fail to come together for worship, we miss the fellowship and friendship of fellow members of the community of faith. We miss the beauty and joy of praying and singing together. We might even miss a significant insight from the preacher. But beyond all these things, we miss receiving renewed assurance of God's promises. We miss hearing again in Scripture, song, and sermon, that word of the Lord which says "I love you, and I will love you forever." We miss our shared response to that word, in confession of sin and of faith and in praise and thanksgiving.

We can certainly exist without worship. We can exist without a lot of things. We could probably retreat into a cave and continue to exist, living off the bugs and rodents we could catch, but we would certainly be missing much of life's meaning and joy. We were not created for that kind of limited life. Nor are we created to live without personal reverence and corporate worship and praise. To live without worship and praise is to live as less than fully human beings. It is to live less than the full and abundant life Christ came to give.

We are grateful that we need not choose between the reasons for Sabbath observance given in Exodus and Deuteronomy. We honor both and see Sabbath observance to be grounded in creation *and* in salvation, both in God's rest *and* God's redemption. Therefore, we thank God for giving us this day for rest and for personal and corporate praise and adoration.

A Blessing not a Burden

We can't leave this commandment without noting a word from Jesus. The gospel of Mark tells about Jesus and his disciples walking beside fields of grain. Some of the disciples plucked heads of grain to eat. That was not considered stealing but, since it was the Sabbath day, the Pharisees complained the disciples were harvesting on the Sabbath, which the Pharisees considered sinful: "Look, why are they doing what is not lawful on the sabbath?" (Mark 2:24) Jesus sums up his reply to their accusation with these words: "The sabbath was made for man, not man for the sabbath; so the Son of man is lord even of the sabbath." (Mark 2:27, 28) The Sabbath, says Jesus, is God's gift for our good. It is given to be a blessing and not a burden. The Sabbath is given to help and not to hinder, to serve and not to enslave.

The next paragraph in Mark's gospel tells of Jesus' encounter with a person who had a withered hand. The Pharisees are watching to see if Jesus will heal on the Sabbath. Jesus invites the man to come to him and asks, "Is it lawful on the sabbath to do good or to do harm, to save life or to kill?" Then Jesus "looked around at them with anger, grieved at their hardness of heart, and said to the man, 'Stretch out your hand.' He stretched it out and his hand was restored." (Mark 3:4, 5) Jesus broke the letter of the law, in order to fulfill the purpose of the law, Since the Sabbath was given for human good, it was right to do good on the Sabbath.

Jesus' Sabbath statement, underscored by his personal action, provides a basic principle that applies to all institutions of life. Lincoln expressed it in terms of government when he spoke of "Government of the people, by the people, and *for* the people." The government is for the people and not just the people for the government. Tyranny results when people become slaves of the government, and the government ceases to serve the people. So also, schools exist for the good of the students, not students for the schools. Hospitals do not exist to provide jobs for doctors and nurses. Hospitals are for the people, not the people for the hospitals.

By word and example, Jesus gives us a third purpose for Sabbath observance. The Lord's Day is for rest and for worship. It is also a day for deeds of caring love. We need rest and refreshment. We need times for praise and worship. We also need freedom from routine responsibilities, in order to carry out the deeds of love and kindness we are created and called, in Christ, to do. The Lord's Day is a time to visit a friend or relative in the hospital, a time to write the letter we have put off writing, a time to make the call that will tell someone that we remember and care, a time to help a neighbor who is in need. To do such work on Sunday is not to sin, but to fulfill this purpose of the Sabbath and of the Lord's Day — "to do good" and "to save life." (Mark 3:4)

We thank God for the gift of the Lord's day. We thank God for the rest and refreshment that come through quiet hours of rest apart from the routine of work. We thank God for the privilege of meeting together for worship and praise. We thank God for time to do deeds of love and caring. We, rightly, thank God, each day for this good gift of one special day in each week of all our days.

Questions and Suggestions for Reflection and Discussion

1. Do you agree the necessity for rest and worship is built into the design of creation? Why? Why not?

2. In what ways do some of us need to "resign from being chairman of the board of the universe"?

3. How are pastors and active church members especially tempted to break this commandment?

4. Why, according to Exodus 20:8-11, did God give the Sabbath and a commandment to keep it holy? Why, according to Deuteronomy 5:12-15? What are we to make of these different reasons? For what good reasons should we observe the sabbath?

5. In what ways is Sabbath observance grounded in both God's rest and God's redemption? Do we sometimes honor the first, while ignoring the second? How do we honor both?

6. Why did the early Christians change from observing Saturday to Sunday? Why is the Christian Sabbath called "the Lord's Day"? (Revelation 1:10)

7. What do we miss when we fail to gather with other Christians on the Lord's Day? What does Mark 2:23 through 3:6 teach us concerning a proper attitude toward, and proper observance of, the Lord's Day?

8. What does "the sabbath was made for man, not man for the sabbath" (Mark 2:27) mean for Sabbath observance? What does it imply concerning other institutions of society?

9. What does "the Son of Man is Lord even of the sabbath" (Mark 2:28) mean for us?

10. What does Jesus' question, "Is it lawful on the sabbath to do good or to do harm, to save life or to kill?" imply concerning the kind of work we are especially encouraged to do on the Sabbath?

Chapter 4

Love, Honor, and
Sometimes Disobey

With the fourth commandment we begin consideration of what is sometimes called the second table of the law. The first three commandments, in the Lutheran/Roman Catholic way of numbering them, deal with our life with God, and the other seven with our life with people. As we begin our journey through these seven commandments, note how they deal concretely with six arenas of life related to (1) relationships with parents and persons of authority, (2) respect and reverence for life, (3) responsible sexuality, (4) dealings with money and property, (5) our use of speech, and (6) our inner attitudes as well as outward actions.

In this chapter, we focus on the Fourth Commandment: "Honor your father and your mother, that your days may be long in the land which the LORD your God gives you." (Exodus 20:12) This commandment says, in effect, "Love, honor, and sometimes disobey." That title is suggested by the marriage vow: "Love, honor, and obey." The "obey" in that statement may seem more appropriate to this commandment than "sometimes disobey" in our title, but please reserve judgment, in that regard, until having read the entire chapter.

Love

All of the commandments, as Jesus reminds us, are fulfilled

through love of God and love of neighbor (see Matthew 32:36-40, Mark 12:28-31, and Luke 10:25-28). Such love has its source in the love of God. "We love because (God) first loved us." (1 John 4:19) To love is to give of oneself for the good of another. "God so loved the world that he gave his only Son, that whoever believes in him should not perish but have eternal life." (John 3:16) In Christ and the Holy Spirit, God still gives himself, in love, to us. In trust and surrender, we love God as we give ourselves to him. As we let God love us, we are liberated to give ourselves, in love, to others.

Those "others" include every person on this planet who can be blessed by our caring. In the specific emphasis of this commandment, they are the particular people within our families and those related to us in positions of authority. We love those in our family/friendship circle when we give them our time and attention, our listening ears and seeing eyes, our caring hearts and helping hands. Jess Lair has said, "The most loving thing we can do is to tell it like it is with us in our deepest hearts."[1] To share, with such openness, is to give ourselves in love. As God, in Christ, has shared what is in his deepest heart, he invites us to share, with him and with those who are closest in family and friendship, what is deepest in ours. It is neither necessary nor wise to engage in such sharing with every person we meet, but in the grace of God we ask for courage to give ourselves, in such love, to those who are nearest and dearest to us.

There is also a proper self-giving love toward those in authority over us and toward the institutions of church, school, business, and state, which they represent. Needless to say, love in these relationships is less intimate and tender than within the circle of family and friendship, but it may be no less self-giving. When we love our country, for example, we will follow John Kennedy's admonition and be concerned not only with what our country can do for us, but with what we can do for our country. In the same way, such love will prompt us to give ourselves to increase and ennoble the worthwhile service of every structure of society with which we are, in any way, involved.

Honor

The fourth commandment specifically charges us to "Honor your father and your mother." Since most of us learned the Ten Commandments in Sunday church school and confirmation classes, we may think that the central message cf this commandment is addressed to children and teenagers. We will next consider that part of its meaning, but will then go on to note that it also speaks to those of us who are older.

To Children and Teenagers

In his *Large Catechism* Luther maintains one of the greatest and best works we can ever do is to honor our parents, even though they are imperfect and make many mistakes. No one in all of human history has had perfect parents. None of us is a perfect parent to our children. Yet, for all their imperfections, parents are the chief channel of God's love to growing children. "Each of us," as psychiatrist Earl Loomis said years ago, "has likely received more love from our parents than we realize. If we hadn't received such love, we probably wouldn't have survived this well this long." As we grow older, and especially from the perspective of years beyond their deaths, we can be more objective about our parents' strengths and weaknesses. It is not difficult for me to list many of my parents' faults and failures, but I continue to thank God that they were, and in memory still are, a mighty means of grace to me.

It is useless to go through life feeling doomed because of having had imperfect parents. We should rather thank God for all the good in our life together, and then trust God for grace to overcome all that has been less than good. Our parents, like ourselves, are sinful and sometimes sick people. Their mistakes, in act and attitude, have left scars in our hearts and memories. They may have hurt us more deeply than anyone else, but, at the same time, they may also have blessed us more than anyone else. We honor them by remembering the blessing, and trusting God for grace to overcome the hurt.

To Persons with Aging Parents

The fourth commandment speaks to young children and teenagers, but its original and more basic message may have been to instruct much older children to honor their elderly and infirm parents and grandparents, who were now dependent on their love and care. We thank God for Social Security and compassionate, competent nursing home care, but are reminded by this commandment that we are not to abandon our elders to the care of the government or a nursing home. Congregations, as well as children, have opportunity for service in this regard. Lively senior citizen groups and "friendly visitor" programs in many congregations are signs that this work of love is being done. But the main responsibility for the care of elderly parents should remain with the children, who continue to give themselves to sustain meaning and joy in the lives of their parents as long as they live. When these responsibilities seem too heavy for us, we do well to ponder this strong biblical admonition: "If anyone does not provide for his relatives, and especially for his own family, he has disowned the faith and is worse than an unbeliever." (1 Timothy 5:8)

Implications for Parents

The "honor" in the parent-child relationship needs to go both ways. It is not only the young who are to honor the older; the older are also to love and respect the younger. Luther stresses this in the *Large Catechism:* "Think not you parents that the parental office is a matter of your pleasure and whim, but remember that God has strictly commanded it and entrusted it to you, and that for the right discharge of its duties you must give an account." The apostle Paul also underscores this mutuality of honor and respect. He says not only, "Children, obey your parents in the Lord, for this is right," but also, "Fathers, do not provoke your children to anger, but bring them up in the discipline and instruction of the Lord." (Ephesians 6:1,4)

Luther also suggests, while it is true, "He who spares the rod hates his son" (Proverbs 13:24), parents should always remember to keep an apple beside the rod to give the child who has done well. That rod, too sternly applied without the apple, can wrongly provoke a child to anger that grows into lifelong resentment. As we look back over our lives, we adults have grateful memories for times of loving correction, but no doubt we remember with equal, if not greater, gratitude times when we received the kind of affirmation and encouragement that is symbolized by Luther's apple. When God says "No" to our sinful desires and spiteful schemes, it is always in order to say "Yes" to our life-fulfillment and lasting joy. "As surely as God is faithful," says the apostle Paul, "our word to you has not been Yes and No. The Son of God, Jesus Christ whom we preached among you . . . was not Yes and No; but in him it is

38

always Yes. For all the promises of God find their Yes in him." (2 Corinthians 1:18-20) Giving an apple of encouragement to a child, or to any human being, is expressive of that great affirmation in Jesus Christ.

It is easy for those of us in the older generation to lament the lack of honor and respect among young people, and those in the younger generation certainly have sins enough to confess. But it may be well for those of us who are older to spend more time confessing the sins of our own generation than those of the next. What have we done by way of positive example to guide those who follow us? We adults decry dishonesty, and then practice deception and deceit in high places. We complain about terrorism and yet, as a nation, depend on violence as the "final solution" to all kinds of economic, social, and political problems, In every political campaign, we wonder whether most of the candidates care more about the next election or the next generation. Are we, as adults, providing an example of high-minded thinking and noble living, or are we rather, by our own dishonorable conduct, tempting the younger generation toward cynicism and even contempt of ourselves and of the institutions of our society?

To cite a personal example, I am grateful to have no memory that my parents ever lied to me. I remember as a pre-schooler going with my parents and twin brother to a Christmas program in the little country school we were soon to attend. Santa Claus was there with gifts for all the children, but there was no deception. Our parents made it clear to us Jesus was for real, but this was only Eddie Monson dressed up in the Santa suit. That honesty did not detract from the fun of Santa's visit, but it did help to enable trust and mutual respect. Our trust is created by the people in whom we have it. As we wish to be trusted, we must be trustworthy, in matters little as well as large. As we wish to be honored, we will seek to be honorable in all our living.

A Word of Promise

As the context of Christ suggests mutuality of honor, so also it suggests mutuality of promise. In both Exodus and Deuteronomy honoring parents is connected with promise: "That your days may be long in the land which the Lord your God gives you" (Exodus 20:12) — "That your days may be prolonged, and that it may go

well with you, in the land which the Lord your God gives you." (Deuteronomy 5:16)[2] As I think of this commandment and of these
promises, I wonder if God doesn't have a parallel commandment
and parallel promise for our time: "Parents, honor your children,
that it may be well with them and that their days may be long on
the earth I have given you." As we live in Christ, we are to live now
in ways that give hope and promise to our children and to generations of their children after them. William Sloan Coffin likes to say,
"What this nation needs is a foreign policy fit for children." We
need policies, domestic and foreign, that do not just impulsively react
to the immediate crisis, but which have the vision to act in the best
interest of the global community for generations yet to be.

Robert McAfee Brown says what the church needs is "a theology fit for children," and urges us to make the fate of children a start-
ing point for our theological reflection. As we think of Jesus' words
about children and see him taking them into his arms to bless them,
it should not be difficult to find a biblical basis for such theology.
If, by our polluting and our wasting, we rob our children and their
children of hope; if, by our warring madness, we deny them the future of promise and blessing that God wills for them — then we are
sinning against our children, far more than they, by rudeness or disrespect, have ever sinned against us.

And Sometimes Disobey

Buttons and bumper stickers sometimes read, "Question Authority." That statement is appropriate. It reminds us all human authority
is under God, and it helps us remember the Fourth Commandment,
like all the commandments, stands under the first: "You shall have
no other Gods before me." Even as we rightly honor parents and
superiors, we let none stand in the place of God. When commanded
to sin we rightly disobey. We then say with Peter and the apostles,
"We must obey God rather than men." (Acts 5:29) When we are
called to go against Christ and conscience, we ask for the courage
of Luther, who defied both state and church when he refused to re-
cant, saying, "Here I stand. I can do no other, so help me God."

Honoring parents does not mean slavish submission to irrational
or immoral authority. There are at least three situations in which
it is right for children to disobey their parents: (1) when commanded
to sin, as when told to lie or steal, (2) when commanded to

engage in activities that are harmful or dangerous, as when told to remove a kite tangled in a power line and (3) when old enough to assume responsibility for oneself, as when a seventeen-year-old decides what to wear to a party, or a thirty-five-year-old decides to marry in spite of parental objections.

"Children," says the apostle Paul, "Obey your parents *in the Lord.*" (Ephesians 6:1; emphasis added) Paul does not say that we are to obey our parents, or any other authorities, *out of the Lord.* When parents, superiors, or governments command us to act in ways we believe to be contrary to the way of Christ and the will of God, when the crowd calls us to sin, when traditions tempt us toward evil, then we pray for courage to stand with Christ and to do the will of God, even when it seems we are standing and acting alone.

For Christians, such disobedience is really divine obedience grounded in the example and teaching of Jesus. As early as age twelve Jesus frightened and dismayed his parents by abandoning the crowd of his kinfolk and acquaintances, in order to hear and question the teachers in the temple. When reprimanded, Jesus referred to an authority higher than his parents, "Did you not know that I must be in my Father's house?" (Luke 2:49)

Jesus is emphatic in affirming an authority higher than any in family relationships: "I have come to set a man against his father, and a daughter against her mother and a daughter-in-law against her mother-in-law; and a man's foes will be those of his own household. He who loves father or mother more than me is not worthy of me; and he who loves son or daughter more than me is not worthy of me." (Matthew 10:35-37) There can be no doubt that for Jesus, divine obedience sometimes meant disobedience even to the honored authority of parents.

When Jesus said, "Then render to Caesar the things that are Caesar's, and to God the things that are God's" (Luke 20:25), it is certain he was not urging his hearers to give Caesar what belongs to God. Some interpreters, such as Colin Morris, suggest Jesus' statement in this text could be translated, "Give Caesar what Caesar's got coming," and that patriotic Jews would have heard this as their descendants might have heard, "Give Hitler what Hitler's got coming," and would have understood it to mean they should not pay taxes to Caesar.[3] One support for this unusual interpretation is found in the accusation brought against Jesus, "We found this man perverting our nation, and forbidding us to give tribute to Caesar."

(Luke 23:2). If Jesus had emphatically affirmed allegiance to Caesar and obedient tax paying, as most interpreters understand Luke 20:25 to mean, it is surprising that he would be accused in the same Gospel of undermining the nation and opposing payment of taxes to Caesar.

Jesus practiced what he preached, and the result was death on the cross. That cross now stands not only as the symbol of our redemption and salvation, but also as a concrete witness to the cost of Christ-like non-conformity in a sinful world. Since there were two thieves crucified with Jesus, we are reminded that sin as well as virtue can lead to suffering. When we experience rejection, it is often because we are more like those thieves than like Jesus. But, we should also remember when we are truly controlled by the love of Christ, we will be out of harmony with many of the ways of the world and will likely be subjected to the ridicule, if not physical punishment, of those who are seeking to maintain the status quo from their positions of privilege and power.

What This World Needs

This world needs a rebirth of proper love and honor for parents and others in authority. Increased respect is due to those who are *authoritative,* but, at the same time, we need courage to stand against those who are only *authoritarian.* We need courage to live with the conscience and conviction of Christ and to oppose principalities and powers, in places high or low, who lure us to live in ways contrary to the life we see in Jesus. This world needs people who will render to Caesar, to parents, and to all in authority, the honor and obedience that is due them, and who, at the same time, will render to God what belongs to God — always remembering that our supreme allegiance, our central loyalty, our basic trust, our very lives, belong to God alone. What this world needs is more people whose consciences are captive neither to Caesar nor to any other human authority, but to Christ — people who see the future as belonging not to those who threaten to destroy it, but to God who wills to bless it — people so confirmed in the conscience, compassion, and courage of Jesus Christ our Lord, that they are enabled to act in divine obedience even when it means disobedience to some human authority. May God help each of us to so love, honor, and sometimes disobey, that we will be among those people.

ENDNOTES

[1]Jess Lair, *I Ain't Much Baby But I'm All I've Got.* Greenwich, CT: Fawcett, 1974, p. 174.

[2]Deuteronomy 11:8-9 relates these promises to the keeping of "all the commandments which I command you this day" and not just to the fourth commandment.

[3]See Colin Morris, *Unyoung — Uncolored — Unpoor.* Abingdon Press, 1969, pp. 111-113.

Questions and Suggestions for
Reflection and Discussion

1. Note how the first three commandments deal with our relationship with God, and the other seven with our life with people. Review the Fourth through Seventh Commandments and note the specific area of human concern with which each deals. What areas of life are neither directly nor indirectly related to any of the Ten Commandments?

2. It has been said "to love is to give oneself" or, more specifically, "to give oneself for the good of another." Do you agree with these definitions? Why? Why not? What other definitions or descriptions can you give?

3. How do your definitions of love relate to keeping the Fourth Commandment?

4. How do we express love toward institutions such as church, school, and state, as well as toward individuals?

5. Why should we honor parents and authorities who sometimes behave dishonorably?

6. Do you agree with Dr. Loomis that each of us has probably received more love than we realize? Discuss the kinds of love we often take for granted.

7. Do you agree our parents both hurt and bless us? How is this possible? What does this mean for you?

8. Do you agree children are not obligated to obey their parents when: (a) commanded to sin? (b) commanded to risk unnecessary danger? and (c) old enough to decide for themselves? Can you suggest other similar situations? When are children old enough to decide for themselves?

9. Do you believe the Fourth Commandment is more important for young children (under 20) in relation to obedience to their parents or to older children (over 40 or 50) in relation to the care of their aging parents? Defend your answer.

10. To what extent are older children justified in depending on Social Security and nursing homes to care for their aging parents rather than providing for them themselves?

11. How are parents to provide proper discipline without provoking their children to anger? What is the place of the rod and the apple?

12. How do we say "Yes" to our children, while saying "No" to their sinful and foolish requests and desires?

13. Is it wrong for parents to lie to their children about things like Santa Claus? Why? Why not?

14. What do calls for foreign policy and theology "fit for children" mean to you? In what ways is it sinful for us to live in a manner that robs our children of their future?

15. When is it right for Christians to disobey civil authorities? What do the teachings and example of Jesus mean for us in this regard?

16. What is the difference between authoritative and authoritarian leaders? How are we to relate to each?

17. When someone says, "I will always obey my country," is this proper patriotism or sinful idolatry? Defend your answer.

18. How does confrontation with this commandment drive us to Christ? What sins does it prompt us to confess? What then do we receive from Christ?

19. What amendment of life does this commandment challenge

us to make?

20. How do we keep, and help each other keep this commandment?

Chapter 5

Practicing the Pro-Life Principle[1]

"You shall not kill." (Exodus 20:13, Deuteronomy 5:17) What did these words mean to those who first heard them, at the time of Moses more than three thousand years ago? How did Jesus understand them, over a thousand years later? What did they mean during the first centuries of Christian history? How do we understand this commandment today? What does it teach and imply concerning the controversial issues of life and death, with which we are often forced to struggle these days?

The Original Meaning

The original meaning of the Fifth Commandment is conveyed by the New English Bible, and similar versions which translate it, "You shall not commit murder." This commandment was originally understood to prohibit all killing, except that which was specifically permitted or, in some cases actually commanded. Animals, for example, could be killed, although their blood was not to be eaten, because it was understood that blood was "its life." (Genesis 9:4) Capital punishment, in certain situations, was not only permitted, but commanded. "Whoever strikes a man so that he dies, shall be put to death . . . Whoever strikes his father or mother shall be put to death . . . Whoever steals a man (that is, takes another person's slave) shall be put to death . . . Whoever curses his father or mother shall be put to death." (Exodus 21;l2, 15-17) Whoever struck his male or female slave with a rod would be punished, not put to death. "But if the slave survives a day or two, he is not to be punished; for the slave is his money." (Exodus 21:21) The general rule was, "You shall give life for life, eye for eye, tooth for tooth, hand for hand, foot for foot, burn for burn, stripe for stripe." (Exodus 21:23-24)

In certain circumstances, killing in war was also specifically commanded. If the people of Israel were attacking a city some distance from home, they were first to offer terms of peace. If those terms were accepted, the people of that city were to become their slaves, but if they refused, the city was to be attacked and all men in the city were to be killed. If the city under attack was close to where the people of Israel were living, the penalty was much more severe. "You shall save nothing alive that breathes, but you shall utterly destroy them." (Deuteronomy 20:16-17) The purpose of such severity was "That they may not teach you to do according to all their abominable practices which they have done in the service of their gods, and so to sin against the Lord your God." (Deuteronomy 20:18) Such teaching prescribes an ancient holocaust that reminds us of a later "final solution" to the problem of racial and religious differences. All the people were to be killed, but the fruit trees were to be spared. "You may eat from them, but you shall not cut them down." (Exodus 20:19) In this practice we see an intimation of the neutron bomb, which is designed to kill people but to spare property.

A Christian Perspective

There is something within us which rebels against some of this teaching. Christians have never practiced everything that is commanded in these verses. I have never heard of a Christian church that advocates killing children who curse their parents. We understand these Old Testament passages in the context of the teaching and example of Jesus. "You have heard that it was said," says Jesus, quoting Exodus 21:24, "An eye for an eye and a tooth for a tooth.' But I say to you, do not resist one who is evil. But if anyone strikes you on the right cheek, turn to him the other also . . . You have heard it was said, 'You shall love your neighbor and hate your enemy.' But I say to you, Love your enemies and pray for those who persecute you . . ." (Matthew 5:38, 39, 43, 45)

Mark says Jesus "declared all foods clean" (Mark 7:19) and the account of Peter's vision in Acts 10:9-29 made it dramatically clear Old Testament regulations concerning unclean foods and unclean people were no longer to be observed. So also, the life and teachings of Jesus clearly reject Old Testament commands that call for

48

vengeance and death. A Christian preacher who advocated con-
cubinage and polygamy, on the basis of a correct Old Testament
interpretation of the Sixth Commandment, would be expelled from
the ministry. Why then do many Christians affirm preachers who
insist on similar Old Testament interpretation of the Fifth Commandment, which is just as clearly at variance with the teachings of Jesus?

Jesus specifically opposed the enforcement of Old Testament passages, such as Leviticus 20:10 and Deuteronomy 22:23-24, requir-
ing capital punishment. The scribes and Pharisees brought a woman
to Jesus who had been "caught in the act of adultery," and they
declared, "Now in the law Moses commanded us to stone such. What
do you say about her?" To which Jesus replied, "Let him who is
without sin among you be the first to throw a stone at her." (John
8:3, 5, 7) Having shamed and dispersed her accusers, Jesus says to
the woman, "Neither do I condemn you." (John 8:11) Jesus saves
her life and, thereby also, gives a warning to all sinners against self-
righteously condemning others to death.

Although some Old Testament passages speak of a time when
"they shall beat their swords into plowshares, and their spears into
pruning hooks; nation shall not lift up sword against nation, neither
shall they learn war any more" (Isaiah 2:4; Micah 4:3), many Old
Testament passages, such as those noted above, advocate killing in
holy war. Jesus, however, did not do so. He said to an impulsive
defender, "Put your sword back into its place; for all who take the
sword will perish by the sword." (Matthew 26:52) Luke's account
of the same event records that Jesus gave an even stronger rebuke:
"No more of this!" (Luke 22:51) For the first three hundred years
of Christian history, most Christians took Jesus' command literally
and refused to kill in war. But, for many centuries, most Lutherans
and Roman Catholics have almost totally ignored Jesus' command
in Luke 22:51, preferring rather to focus on Luke 22:19-20, where
Jesus speaks of his sacramental body and blood. We can only wonder
how the history of Europe and of the world would have been different, if all Lutherans and Roman Catholics had taken both passages
with equal seriousness.

Jesus' New Understanding

Jesus' teaching gives us a new understanding of the Fifth Commandment. He calls us to reject violence and revenge and to love

even our enemies. To underscore this teaching, Jesus practiced what he preached. He lived the way of the cross. Jesus chose to suffer rather than to inflict suffering. He chose to die rather than to kill. "I came," he says, "that they may have life, and have it abundantly." (John 10:10) He gave his life to give us life. In Christ — in his teaching, in his living, in his death on the cross, in his resurrection — we are assured that God is on the side of life. In Christ we know God comes to bless, to enable, and to fulfill life.

Jesus let nothing stand in the way of life-giving action. In our consideration of the Third Commandment we noted how Jesus broke the letter of the Sabbath law in order to fulfill its life-giving purpose. With Jesus, people came first. Jesus lived according to a pro-people, pro-life principle.

In Christ we are called to be pro-life and pro-people. We are to refrain from all that degrades and destroys life. We are to do all that we can to enrich and ennoble life. We are to be for every good thing — for all healing, for all learning, for all that is beautiful in music and art, for all of everything that gives meaning and joy to life. We are to help and not to hurt. We are to give life and not to destroy it. We are to live with what Albert Schweitzer called "reverence for life." We are to stand against all that would stifle and smother life.

Complex Issues of Life and Death

Few Christians would disagree with such general statements, but when we come to their specific application to concrete issues of life and death, we are quickly embroiled in complex and controversial questions. Equally sincere Christians come down on different sides of issues such as abortion, capital punishment, euthanasia, suicide, and Christian participation in war. None of us can claim to have a final word on these matters, but we must seek to stand with Christ on each of them. I am, therefore, bold to share some present reflections concerning what this commandment has come to mean for me, in relation to these controversial issues of life and death. I share these convictions in an attempt to be consistent with the pro-life principle that we see in Jesus.

Abortion

Through counseling experience, I know some of the anguish of those who wrestle with the problem of unwanted pregnancy. Perhaps no man, not even the father, can ever fully understand and feel that anguish. I have heard women tell of both the sense of relief and also of the regret that has followed the decision to have an abortion. We are not to stand in self-righteous judgment against any person who has made this decision. As we all live in constant need of God's forgiveness and mercy, none of us is to condemn or to cast the first stone.

But, at the same time, I find it impossible to limit reverence for life to the born and to the viable unborn, and am deeply troubled over statistics reporting a million and a half abortions per year in the United States, and millions more around the world. Some believe that one-fourth of all American pregnancies now end in abortion. My personal disdain for abortion is no doubt related to the fact that our first child was born four months prematurely and lived only one hour. I can vividly recall standing with the doctor by the incubator as we watched a little girl who weighed only one pound, thirteen ounces, as she struggled for life. "She cannot live," the doctor said. "Had she been a month further along she might have had a chance of one in ten." If she had been born today, new techniques might have saved her life. We were deeply grieved by her death. She was not just a piece of tissue. She was a baby girl. I wonder if all who choose to "terminate a pregnancy" realize what they are doing. However we may differ concerning the personal, religious, ethical and legal issues that are involved in abortion, must we not agree that taking the life of the unborn is, at best, an awesome and agonizing business which should never be taken lightly?

There are times, such as to save the life of the mother, when abortion is a tragic necessity, but it never should be seen as simply another method of birth control. To say, or even to think, "Don't worry, you can always have an abortion," reveals neither love nor reverence for life. As we stand against abortion, we rightly stand for responsible sexuality, responsible sex education, and responsible contraception. We support everything that helps to prevent unwanted pregnancy and which thus makes it unnecessary to even consider abortion. The Roman Catholic Church's official opposition to birth control is a hindrance rather than help in this regard. Would that they were as strongly for responsible contraception as they are against irresponsible abortion.

For many women, abortion has become an issue of personal power, freedom, and dignity. They do not desire to have abortions, but they refuse to live under the dictation of male dominance. "Abortion rights" has become a symbol of essential liberation. The pro-life principle suggests that, while the yearning for freedom and fulfillment is correct, the selection of this symbol is wrong. Agreeing that there are justifiable abortions is one thing; claiming a legal or moral right to an abortion in all circumstances is something else. No one has an inherent right to end the life of another. Fathers and husbands do not have the right to dominate, let alone destroy, the lives of their daughters and wives. Nor do mothers have an unlimited right to end the lives of their unborn at any stage of development. True freedom and liberation for the women of the world can be achieved only through the kind of responsible sexuality on the part of both men and women that makes it unnecessary to consider abortion. As pro-life people, we are called in Christ to do everything in our power to achieve that goal.

Capital Punishment

To my mind, capital punishment is clearly contrary to the teaching of Jesus that only the sinless were to participate in executions. If that rule were followed, there would, needless to say, be no capital punishment. I have sometimes said, in jest, that I am personally so strongly opposed to the death penalty, I believe that all who support it should be taken out and shot! Capital punishment is, however, no joking matter. It is, in my opinion, an institutionalized and legalized form of murder, human sacrifice, and deliberate violence which, by example, teaches violence rather then deters it. Many studies show that capital punishment does not deter crime (some suicidal murderers, such as Gary Gilmore, may even have committed their crimes *because* of capital punishment), but, even if it did, I would still oppose it. We might deter thievery by branding the word "thief" into the forehead of thieves or by cutting off their hands. We reject such means of deterrence as cruel and barbaric. But are they more barbaric than cutting off people's lives by capital punishment?

Euthanasia

Reverence for life also compels me to stand in basic opposition to euthanasia or mercy killing. Heroic measures to extend life in ways that degrade the person are not required. Since the person has already died, situations of brain death do not involve mercy killing. When the brain is dead, it is neither necessary nor desirable to maintain biological function through external support. But reverence for life *does* call us to care for people who are limited through illness, accident, or retardation. As with abortion, there may be tragic circumstances in which reverence for life necessitates an exception to the general rule of life preservation. Gandhi, the great advocate of compassion and nonviolence, believed that if his child were in the agony of terminal rabies, and there were no medical relief available, it might be his duty to take the child's life. We thank God that the availability of pain-killers now makes it unnecessary to consider killing a child in such circumstances. But even if we can imagine some other situation in which we believe euthanasia to be the will of God, we need to beware lest the tragic exception become accepted as the general rule. With mercy killing, as with abortion, capital punishment and war, the real problem is not in the tragically necessary exceptional circumstance, but in the institutionalized killing that transforms the exceptions into established practice.

Suicide

We do not condemn those who have taken their own lives. Some of these have died of an illness of mind or emotion as real as any sickness that afflicts the body. Whatever the circumstances, we can only entrust each one to the mercy of God. At the same time, Jesus' pro-life principle calls us to do all in our power to prevent suicide. Some say, "People have freedom, let them kill themselves if they want to." The fact is, however, almost everyone who is prevented from committing suicide is later deeply grateful to be alive. Therefore, we commit ourselves to do all we can, not only to prevent suicide but also to help people through situations which prompt them to consider it.

War

Except for those who lived during the first three hundred years after Christ (which was a very long time!), most Christians have given uncritical and often enthusiastic support of killing in war. We have, in effect, often taken the cross by the short end and sharpened the other into a sword. For hundreds of years, many Christians also supported the institution of slavery. We now see that support to have been a mistake and a sin. By sound and silence, the majority of the

Christian church still supports the institution of war. Yet modern warfare could· produce more death and suffering in a single hour than all the horrors of slavery across the centuries. If it was a sin to support the institution of slavery, is it not now a sin to support the institution of war?

We need responsible police power in a sinful world. But we do not need the kind of tribal morality that makes it criminal to kill a fellow American, but regards it as heroic patriotism to kill (or plan to kill or help pay to kill) millions of foreigners who have been labeled "the enemy." Killing millions for peace and freedom is as ironic and immoral as would be lying and stealing for the sake of honesty, or even raping to promote chastity.

In his presentation of the Fifth Commandment in the *Large Catechism,* Luther accepts the state's right to execute criminals and to conduct war. He says that what is forbidden to individuals is not forbidden to civil government, which he believed was acting in the place of God in killing criminals and waging war. But we must ask, as did Leo Tolstoy: If it is wrong for an individual or small group to kill, how many does it take in order to form a government with the right to kill? If it is wrong for one or ten or one hundred, what makes it inherently right for one thousand, ten thousand, or a million?[2] We also note what happened in Luther's beloved Germany when the state's right to kill was fully exercised. The government began to act as if it were God, and the horrors of the Second World War and Hitler's holocaust were the result.

One of the tests of the morality of any attitude or action is to observe the consequences. "Every sound tree," said Jesus, "bears good fruit, but the bad tree bears evil fruit . . . Thus you will know them by their fruits." (Matthew 7:17, 20) What is the fruit of reliance upon the institution of war? We fought world wars to end war and to make the world safe for democracy. We are now engaged in the greatest arms race in human history. The United States now has thirty thousand nuclear weapons, many far more deadly than the bombs dropped on Hiroshima and Nagasaki. We have plans to build thousands more over the next few years. What is the end of this road on which we are traveling? If thirty thousand nuclear weapons are not enough, will fifty thousand be enough? One hundred thousand? We don't cure our headaches by cutting off our heads! Do we really believe that we can save America by destroying the world?

In the *Large Catechism* Luther also says that if we see an innocent person under sentence of death and fail to do all we can to rescue that person, it will be no excuse to say we didn't will that person's
death. We will be responsible and guilty for his death. Reading that,
I wonder what Luther would say if he had lived through the world
wars of our century and could see the arms race we are in today.
Would he not stand as strongly against idolatrous militarism in our
time as he stood against idolatrous ecclesiasticism in his own? Would
he not take his stand, and call us to stand with him, on behalf of
those innocent millions, and even hundreds of millions, of God's
children who would perish in the holocaust of a nuclear war which
would be a thousand times worse than anything Hitler could have
devised or even imagined?

More than twenty-five years ago President Eisenhower, who was
certainly no pacifist, was deeply troubled by the already expanding
arms race. He warned against the acquisition of unwarranted influence by the military-industrial complex. He declared that excessive military spending robbed the poor and oppressed the needy.
Then he stated his hope that, one day, the people of this planet would
get so fed up with the warring madness of many of their leaders they
would rise up to demand peace instead of war, life instead of death.

Today as we confess Christ, the Prince of Peace and Lord of
Life, we ask ourselves, "What are we waiting for?" Do we need
to wait until the bombs begin to go off before we take our stand
for peace? Then all who survive will surely ask, "Why didn't some-
body do something to prevent this horror?" Christ calls us *now* to
love our enemies. He calls us to take up our cross, to put down the
sword, and to follow him. Christ calls us to live out the pro-life principle, to live with reverence for life, to work for a world of peace
and justice, not only for ourselves and for our children but for generations upon generations yet to be.

There are Christian alternatives to war. We are to create peace
through justice. Non-violent means of reconciliation and global structures for international security can replace our warring madness. As
people of Christ, we renounce the sword and affirm the way of the
cross. As members of a worldwide community in Christ, we reject
nationalistic tribalism and seek to live as citizens of one world. In
Christ, we are called to be the vanguard of a new humanity. In Christ,
we seek to learn of the apostle Paul and from people like Gandhi
and Martin Luther King, Jr. to not "be overcome by evil," but to

"overcome evil with good." (Romans 12:21)

Jesus' pro-life principle calls us to consistent affirmation of life, consistent efforts to do all we can to enhance and enable life, consistent efforts to stand against all that would degrade and destroy life. "You shall not kill," says the Fifth Commandment. "You shall love and give life," says Jesus. May the love of God so grasp, heal, and control us that we will live from this day forward with deeper and wider reverence for life. May God, whose love gives life, enable us to be consistently pro-life in all our living.

ENDNOTES

[1]For a more complete development of the themes of this chapter, see the author's *Pro-Life/Pro-Peace*. Minneapolis: Augsburg Publishing House, 1986.

[2]*The Kingdom of God and Peace Essays.* London: Oxford University Press, 1974, p. 14.

Questions and Suggestions for
Reflection and Discussion

1. Is all killing murder? When is killing *not* murder? When *is* it murder?

2. Study the Old Testament references where killing is commanded noted at the beginning of Chapter 5. Why hasn't the Christian church followed these teachings? What (or who?) gives us the authority to disobey these commandments?

3. Do you agree God is on the side of life and we are "called to be pro-life and pro-people"? What does John 10:10 teach us in this regard? What does it mean to live with "reverence for life"?

4. Most Christians, since the fourth century, have maintained there are tragic exceptional circumstances in which the taking of life is justifiable. Does this give anyone the "right" to take life when desiring to do so? Discuss the difference between taking life in exceptional circumstances and the institutionalized acceptance of killing.

5. When is abortion justifiable? When is it not? Does a woman have a "right" to an abortion? Do the unborn have any rights? Are "abortion rights" a good symbol of Christian feminism? Why? Why not?

6. Is the Roman Catholic church correct in opposing both contraception and abortion? Why? Why not?

7. What does John 8:1-11 teach us concerning capital punishment? Do the teachings and example of Jesus support Christian advocacy of the death penalty? Why? Why not?

8. What is the difference between passive and active euthanasia? Are Christians ever justified in practicing either? If so, when? If not, why not?

9. How are we to regard those who have committed suicide? Are we justified in attempting to prevent someone from committing suicide? Why? Why not?

10. What is the difference between police power and military power? What is the purpose of each? Under what law and under what limits does each operate? Can we consistently support one while opposing the other?

11. How many people are needed to organize a government with authority to kill people in warfare? Do governments have an absolute authority to kill people? Why? Why not?

12. Is there any evil in the world that justifies the use of weapons which threaten the destruction of humanity? Can we save America by destroying the world? If it would be a sin to use such weapons, is it also a sin to possess them and to threaten their use?

13. What does Jesus' "No more of this!" (Luke:22:51) rejection of the use of the sword mean for us? Would the human prospect be better or worse if Christians were to practice this teaching?

14. Discuss Christian alternatives to violence and war. What is the place of reconciliation? Of global security? Of commitment to justice? Of the non-violent way of the cross? What does Jesus' cross teach us concerning another way of confronting evil?

15. Can we defeat the devil with the devil's weapons? How are we to overcome evil with good?

16. How does confrontation with this commandment drive us to Christ? What sins does it prompt us to confess? What then do we receive from Christ?

17. What amendment of life does this commandment challenge us to make?

18. How do we keep, and help each other keep, this commandment?

Chapter 6

Sacramental Sex

Each of the Ten Commandments is a gift for our good. These ten are given to bless us, to enable our joy, and to help us give joy to others.

The Ten Commandments also seek to preserve and enhance other good gifts God has given us. We need to look behind the negative, "You shall not," in most of the commandments, to the positive treasures they seek to preserve. Think, for example, of the three commandments sometimes described as the pillars on which our society rests. Although stated negatively, each guards a positive good. The Fifth Commandment, "You shall not kill," seeks to preserve and enhance the gift of life. The Seventh Commandment, "You shall not steal," teaches respect for, and the right use of, the material things which we call "goods." The Sixth Commandment, "You shall not commit adultery," on which we focus in this chapter, seeks to preserve and enhance the good gift of our sexuality. It is intended to help us live in ways that make this gift the blessing God created it to be.

Therefore, we begin our consideration of the Sixth Commandment by following Martin Luther's example of being positive about it. Most of Luther's explanations of the commandments, included in the *Small Catechism,* are stated both negatively and positively. The Fifth Commandment, for example, means "negatively" that we should not hurt our neighbor and "positively" that we should help our neighbor in all physical needs. But when Luther comes to the Sixth Commandment his meaning is entirely positive — *"You shall not commit adultery.* What does this mean for us? We are to fear and love God so that in matters of sex, our words and conduct are pure and honorable and husband and wife love and respect each other."

Luther follows the lead of the New Testament in understanding the Sixth Commandment to mean more than it did in the Old Testament. It may have originally related more to matters of property than to "matters of sex" and was understood to mean "another man's wife is his property and you are to leave her alone." King David, for example, is reprimanded by Nathan the Prophet for having taken Bathsheba and arranged for her husband's murder. David stole another man's wife, which was a great and grievous sin. But it was apparently not considered sinful for David to have many other wives and concubines (see 2 Samuel 3:2-5, 5:13, 15:16). Solomon is reported to have had "700 wives, princesses, and 300 concubines" and is criticized because "his wives turned away his heart" to other gods, but *not* for breaking the Sixth Commandment. (1 Kings 11:3) Our chief concern, therefore, is not only with what the commandment originally meant, but with what it means for us today in the context of Christ and the New Testament.

Why This Commandment?

When asked, "Did God give us the Sixth Commandment because sex is bad?" some confirmation students answer, "Yes, it must be bad or there wouldn't be a commandment against it." We then need to point out the commandment is not "against sex," but against *adultery* and we have been given the Sixth Commandment not because sex is bad but because it is good. God wills our human fulfillment, including our sexual fulfillment, and is therefore against everything that messes up our relationships and hinders that fulfillment.

We need to see both this commandment and our sexuality in the context of creation and of Christ. The last paragraph of Genesis, Chapter 1, says God created human beings male and female. They were to be fruitful and fill the earth. God gives them the earth as a garden in which to live. Then it says, 'God saw everything that he had made, and behold it was very good." (Genesis 1:31) Our sexuality is among the "very good" gifts God has given to us.

As Christians, we believe God has blessed us with this gift, not only to enable us to have children but also as a means of sharing love and joy in the relationship of marriage. Although we do not consider marriage a sacrament, there is a sense in which we can say our sexuality is intended to be sacramental. A sacrament is a visible, concrete, personal means of grace. We believe God intends our sexual relations to be a means of grace and love. As holy communion is a sacramental means of renewing our life with God and the Christian community, so sexual relations are designed to be a sacramental means of loving and gracious renewal between husband and wife.

Since sexual relations are not only for conceiving children, we believe those means of family planning which are not physically harmful are the gift of God. Someone has suggested the only commandment humanity has kept is the one that says, "Be fruitful and multiply and fill the earth." (Genesis 1:28) We are grateful the fulfillment of that command has come to the time when safe methods of contraception are available to enable both sexual fulfillment and responsible family planning.

Faithfulness, Freedom, and Fulfillment

Faithfulness, freedom, fulfillment: these three words capture much of the central meaning of the Sixth Commandment. They go together: faithfulness enables the freedom in which fulfillment is possible. It seems, to some, that the Sixth Commandment's call to faithfulness limits our freedom. In one sense it does. It cancels our freedom to be promiscuous and to get involved in superficial relationships which often end in misery and regret. But, in a more profound sense, it is faithfulness that enables freedom. When are we really free — free to be ourselves, free to be honest, free to give ourselves in the abandonment of love and caring to another person, free to be loved and love? That kind of freedom is possible only in a relationship of faithfulness, where we know someone loves and cares for us. That faithfulness sets us free, and in that freedom we find fulfillment.

The sex researchers, Masters and Johnson, who are not noted for being either pious or prudish in sexual matters, have said it is not faithfulness but promiscuity that is ultimately boring. They believe that "the pleasure bond" is commitment. Loyalty, love, faithfulness — these add up to the kind of commitment that makes true sexual freedom and fulfillment possible.

In the Context of Grace

As with every other dimension of love, it is essential we see our sexuality in the context of grace. There is a significant connection between grace and sexual fulfillment. If counseling experience and reading give an accurate indication, there must be millions who need to bring their sexuality into the realm of grace. We Christians have been taught, since childhood, that we cannot save ourselves by doing good works, yet there are many who are trying to save themselves sexually by their good works. Captured by some ideal of sexual performance, they are working hard to achieve joy and ecstasy. Such self-centered effort is like trying hard to fall asleep. The harder we try, the more it eludes us. Many sexual problems are the direct result of such performance anxiety.

David and Vera Mace, who write profoundly of marriage from a Christian perspective, suggest that, while we may need to work at certain aspects of our marriages such as communication, handling hostility, money management, and child rearing, we should not work at our sexual relationship. We should love at it and play at it, but not *work* at it. Grace saves us from such self-saving work. Grace does not demand achievement by ourselves or our partners. Grace gives freedom in which to love with abandon and caring. In the context of grace, we do not seek to perform or to prove anything. Grace frees us to lose ourselves in giving and receiving love and, at the same time, to be surprised by joy and gladness.

The atmosphere of every room in the house should be the atmosphere of grace. Grace should abound when the cake collapses in the kitchen or a mistake is made in the workshop. When grace abounds in the bedroom, it becomes a place of joyous celebration of love. We therefore thank God for the good gifts of our sexuality and of his grace, which together are creative of such celebration.[1]

Significant Sexual Questions

By implication, the Sixth Commandment speaks to contemporary sexual questions that are frequently raised in the context of pastoral counseling. These issues are as significant for some people as they are controversial for others. None of us has any final word from the Lord on these matters. My answers to these questions attempt to be true to both the meaning of this commandment and to the purpose and place of our sexuality, as understood in Christ.

What About Lustful Looking?

"You have heard that it was said," says Jesus as he brings new understanding to this commandment, " 'You shall not commit adultery.' But I say to you that everyone who looks at a woman lustfully has already committed adultery with her in his heart." (Matthew 5:27) This statement is a great leveler. It reminds us that we may be more equally in need of forgiveness for sin against this commandment than a record of actions alone would indicate. When we put these words alongside Jesus' statement to those who would stone the woman taken in adultery; "Let him who is without sin among you be the first to throw a stone at her" (John 8:7), we are guarded against self-righteous pride and arrogant judgment of others.

Jesus' words about lust do not condemn healthy sexual desire. He judges those who look "lustfully," not those who look lovingly or admiringly or even interestedly. There is a fine line between each of those healthy attitudes and sinful lust, but there is a difference. When we are hungry, it is not sinful to salivate at the sight of food. Nor is it sinful to be sexually attracted to another person. But when healthy attraction is infected with greedy, loveless lust, it becomes sinful. Lust seeks only to get and to selfishly enjoy. Love seeks to give and to share joy. Jesus does not condemn us for being human. Our sin is not in having blood pressure, hunger, or sexual interest, but in our greedy and exploitative lovelessness. We, therefore, affirm sexual desire as the good gift of a loving God, ask mercy for our lustfulness, and seek healing to be cleansed of it.

What About Premarital Sex?

The commitment of faithfulness does not begin on the wedding day. In Christ, we are called to be faithful to the person we may one day marry even before we meet that person. When counseling, I am sometimes a little surprised to discover some people, who acknowledge having had many sexual partners, are now very disturbed over the fact that their fiancee or marriage partner has had similar experiences. I believe these feelings witness not only to jealousy, but also to the fact that faithfulness is essential to every loving relationship. It is not just something imposed on us by the Bible. The Bible exposes the reality of essential faithfulness.

Many years ago I was visited by a troubled young man who

confessed to having had many sexual relationships. He had told his current partner that they were both free to have sexual relations with others. But now he was extremely fearful and distressed over the possibility that she might have had sexual relations with someone else. "I can't understand my feelings," he said, "I was the one who insisted on sexual freedom. I don't know what's the matter with me. I can't understand it. I think I must be in love with that girl!" Very interesting! When love entered, when he began to care for her as a person and not just as a plaything, promiscuity went out the window and faithfulness became important. He began to see sexual relations are a sacramental seal of a special relationship of love and commitment.

What About Living Together Without Legal Marriage?

There are complex issues here. What does the Bible mean by marriage? What constitutes marriage? Some say, sometimes cynically, but always correctly, that "marriage is not just a piece of paper or a formal ceremony." But, whatever marriage is not, Christian marriage *does* involve personal commitment and public declaration of love and faithfulness to one another. Some claim that although they are not legally married, they do have a relationship of love and commitment under God far deeper than many who are legally married. They may even say "We think we are married in the sight of God." But, if that is true, "Why not get legally married?" To which some reply, "We know so many bad marriages we are afraid getting married will ruin our wonderful relationship." Rightly understood, marriage is not a curse but a blessing. Dietrich Bonhoeffer may overstate the case when he says, "It is not your love that sustains the marriage, but from now on, the marraige that sustains your love."[2] Marriage is sustained by love; but the reverse is also true. Love is sustained by marriage. It is well we can't just walk off and forget each other on a moment's notice. The legal obligations about which we may sometimes complain give us a framework of security in which we can be more free and honest with each other. They keep us together through troubled days and give us time to be renewed again in love toward one another.

Therefore, it is my conviction that those who have the commitment, love, and loyalty central to marriage should get married, and those who do not have that kind of commitment should not live together and that they are risking great grief in doing so. Such relationships are frequently fraught with fear, tension, and difficulty, including frequent problems hindering sexual fulfillment. Living together or engaging in premarital relations as a test of sexual compatibility is like testing a parachute by jumping out of a fifth story window. The conditions are not right. The right conditions are present only in a relationship of personal and public commitment in which it is no longer necessary to test anything.

What About Extramarital Sex

Some have said, in counseling, that they thank God for the meaning and joy of an extramarital relationship. Many more have told of their misery and regret. On balance, counseling experience confirms my commitment to the importance of marital fidelity. Here also, we think of the kind of faithfulness that makes fulfillment possible. There is a proper openness in every loving marriage — openness to grow, openness to our partner's involvement in activities we may not enjoy. But granting all that, our sexuality remains the sacrament of a special relationship. To become sexually involved with someone else is not only against God and the Bible, it is against our partner and the relationship we share.

As married people, we need to do all in our power to make it as easy as possible for us to trust each other. Trust is not something we can decide to have. Trust doesn't happen because I resolve to try to trust my wife today. If I have to do that, something is wrong. Our trust is created by the people in whom we have it. If we live in trust, it is because we have lived together in ways that enable and sustain that trust. To be trusted, we must either be cleverly deceitful or truly trustworthy. Given that choice, the way of love and wisdom is not hard to select. May God give us the strength to live it.

What About Sexual Fulfillment for Single Persons?

In response to this question, which is frequently raised in counseling by students and young adults, we in the church have often replied with either negatives or with silence. Neither has been sufficiently helpful, and we should try to do better. Someone should write a book called *Sexual Fulfillment for Single Persons in a Christian Context*. I don't know everything that should be in that book, but

I am sure it would stress we need not be married to have full,
meaningful, and joyful lives. I am sure it would affirm the full humanity of celibate living and would not advocate promiscuity or loveless, irresponsible sexuality of any kind. I am sure it would speak
of the profound personal fulfillment which comes through in-depth
relationships which do not include sexual activity, and it would speak
frankly of both the fulfillment and frustration of varying degrees
of physical involvement in dating relationships.

I believe such a book would speak a good word on behalf of sexual self-fulfillment as a gift and blessing from God and not just as
a horrible, unmentionable sin. It would likely point out as does James
Nelson in his book *Embodiment* that the sin of Onan in Genesis
38:7-10 does not relate, as is often believed, to masturbation, but
to Onan's refusal to fulfill the command, of that time, to father a
child by his brother's widow. That account, as Nelson points out,
also reflects an ancient misunderstanding of reproduction which understood his act to be the equivalent of abortion.[3] Thank God we
now know better.

God has created our sexuality and has given this wonderful gift
to people who are single as well as married. We should beware of
all sexual attitudes and activities that are harmful to ourselves or
to others but, at the same time, need to be open to the possibility
that sexual fulfillment is possible in more than one way. God's gift
of sexuality can be a means of fulfillment for single persons as well
as to those who are married.

What About Homosexuality?

What does the Bible say about it? The Bible clearly condemns
lustful and sinful homosexual behavior. But the Bible does not relate to the vital distinction between sexual orientation and sexual behavior. Nor are there Scripture passages that speak directly to the
situation of persons of the same sex who are in committed loving
relationships.

The only essential difference between homosexuals and heterosex-
uals is that homosexuals discover themselves to be primarily attracted
sexually to persons of the same sex. We do not choose whether we
are going to be sexually interested in persons of the same or opposite sex. This is not just a matter of personal preference. Sexual orientation is similar to being left or right-handed or to being blind to

66

certain colors. We do not choose it, it is something that is given to us. In understanding homosexuality, it is essential to keep this fact in mind. Being of homosexual orientation is, in itself, no more sinful than being left-handed or color-blind.

Whatever our sexual orientation, we are to live responsibly and morally with the desires we have received. When we begin to understand homosexuality we are forced to ask, "Should people of homosexual orientation be judged by different standards than those who are heterosexual?" Sexual morality is not just a matter of actions; it is a matter of relationships, commitment, loyalty, and love. Certainly there are sinful homosexual, as well as heterosexual, relationships, attitudes, and actions. Can there also be moral sexual relationships between committed and loving persons of homosexual, as well as heterosexual, orientation? The biblical passages which clearly condemn lustful and exploitative homosexual behavior do not speak directly to this question. Some, who are deeply committed to Jesus Christ, confess to having found meaning and fulfillment in such relationships, which they believe would be impossible with persons of the opposite sex. They may be mistaken. To hear them sincerely thank God for such fulfillment may shock and disturb us, but it can also help us to be more compassionately understanding and less self-righteously judgmental.

What About Divorce and Remarriage of Divorced Persons?

Divorce is usually a grievous and difficult experience, which is sometimes more painful than if one's partner had died. To marry with dreams of love, joy, and fulfillment, and then to have those dreams come crashing down in the dust and ashes of divorce, is often one of life's most agonizing experiences.

In Old Testament times, divorce was legally easy for men, but impossible for women. If, after marriage, a husband discovered his wife had "no favor in his eyes because he found some indecency in her," he could write "her a bill of divorce" and send "her out of his house." (Deuteronomy 24:1)

Jesus, however, has some very strong things to say against divorce and remarriage of divorced persons. In Mark 10:10-12 and Luke 16:18, both divorce and remarriage are virtually forbidden. In Matthew 5:31-32 and 19:9, Jesus makes an exception in situations involving "unchastity." When questioned by his disciples concerning the severity of his statement opposing divorce, Jesus replied, "Not all men can receive this saying . . . he who is able to receive this, let him receive it." (Matthew 19:11,12) These words remind us to be compassionate and gracious, rather than legalistic, in our understanding and application of Jesus' teaching. Jesus said, "The sabbath was made for man, not man for the sabbath." (Mark 2:27) The same is true of all institutions of society, including marriage. Marriage was made for people, not people for marriage. Marriage is another of God's gifts for our good. It is given to bless and not to enslave us. Understanding Jesus' teachings compassionately, as he invites us to do, opens the possibility of appropriate divorce and remarriage of divorced persons.

Divorce should always be a last resort. Every troubled couple should seek help in facing and correcting their problems before considering divorce. In God's forgiveness and the healing power of his Holy Spirit, there are possibilities for new beginnings in life together. But, as someone has said, when a marriage is dead, and the relationship is hurtful to everyone involved, the only respectable solution may be to have a funeral for it. When divorced persons seek to enter a new marriage relationship that holds promise of mutual fulfillment and upon which we can properly invoke God's blessing, I believe it is right for a Christian pastor to perform the wedding and to ask God's blessing upon their life together.

Where Sin Abounds

Our sexuality is the gracious gift of a loving God. We thank God for the Sixth Commandment and for all else that helps to enhance and ennoble this gift. As men and women, and as husbands and wives, we are, in many ways, faithless to God and to each other. Yet God remains faithful. God still loves us. Grace of mercy and forgiveness abounds to cover our sexual as well as other sins. God's grace makes each day a time of new beginning, new promise, and new possibilities for fulfillment. May we so live in this great love of God, that we are enabled, more and more, to live with love and faithfulness toward God and toward one another. May we be enabled by the spirit of God to be not only forgiven but also forgiving, and to be used by God to be a means of grace, love, and joy to all whose lives touch ours.

68

ENDNOTES

[1]For further thoughts on this subject see Charlie and Martha Shedd, *Celebration in the Bedroom*. Waco, TX: Word Books, 1979; and the chapter "Alone Together" in Lowell and Carol Erdahl, *Be Good to Each Other: An Open Letter on Marriage*. San Francisco: Harper and Row, 1981.

[2]*Letters and Papers from Prison*, Revised Edition, originally published as *Prisoner for God*, Eberhardt Bethge, editor. New York: Macmillan, 1967, p. 49.

[3]James Nelson, *Embodiment*. Minneapolis, MN: Augsburg Publishing House, 1978, p. 168.

Questions and Suggestions for
Reflection and Discussion

1. Do you agree this commandment may have originally had more to do with the husband's property rights concerning his wife than with sexual purity? If this is true, what does it suggest concerning the importance of understanding this commandment, and all commandments, in the context of Christ?

2. Why did God give us the gift of our sexuality? What are the purposes of sexual relations? Why did God give us the Sixth Commandment?

3. If sexual relations are not only for conceiving children, what does this imply concerning Christian attitudes toward conception and family planning?

4. Does Christian commitment to faithfulness help or hinder prospects for sexual fulfillment? Defend your answer.

5. What is the relationship between the Christian gospel of grace and sexual fulfillment?

6. What is the difference between healthy, holy, sexual attraction and sinful, lustful looking?

7. Do you agree "in Christ we are called to be faithful to the person we may one day marry even before we meet that person"? Why? Why not?

8. Do you agree "sexual relations are a sacramental seal of a special relationship of love and commitment"? Why? Why not? What does this imply concerning premarital and extramarital relations?

9. What is your opinion of the practice of people living together without marriage? Do you agree with those who claim to be married in the sight of God without legal marriage? Why? Why not?

10. What do you say to those who express the fear that "getting married may ruin our wonderful relationship"?

11. In what ways is it true that marriage is a blessing that sustains love between husband and wife?

12. Do you agree "living together in order to test sexual compatibiliay is like testing a parachute by jumping out a fifth story window"? Why? Why not?

13. To what extent should a marriage be "open"? To what extent "closed"? Do you agree "our trust is created by the people in whom we have it"? What does this imply for the development and maintenance of trust in marriage?

14. Is it possible for single Christians to experience sexual fulfillment? If so, how? Is sexual self-fulfillment (masturbation) always sinful? Sometimes? Why? Why not?

15. Is sexual morality, and immorality, more a matter of actions or relationships? Are some acts always sinful? Is an action in one relationship holy, in another sinful? If so, what makes the difference?

16. What is the difference between sexual orientation and sexual behavior? What is the essential difference between a heterosexual person and a homosexual person?

17. Is it sinful to be a person of homosexual orientation? Can there be proper sexual relationships between commited and loving persons of homosexual as well as heterosexual orientation. Why? Why not? Do the biblical passages which condemn lustful, exploitative homosexual activity speak directly to such questions?

18. Is it ever justifiable for Christians to be divorced and to become remarried? If so, when is it justifiable? When not?

19. How does confrontation with this commandment drive us to Christ? What sins does it prompt us to confess? What then do we receive from Christ?

20. What amendment of life does this commandment challenge us to make?

21. How do we keep, and help one another keep, this commandment?

Chapter 7

The Place of Possessions

We have noted that the Ten Commandments have meanings beyond the understanding of those who originally received them. Some of their implications also go far *beyond* those of which we are usually aware. This is certainly true of the Seventh Commandment. It seems so simple: "You shall not steal." (Exodus 20:15) The meaning appears obvious — don't rob, shoplift, or swindle — and by not doing such you will have kept this commandment. Since most of us probably haven't done much thieving or swindling lately, we may feel confident that we have obeyed this commandment. But when we think beyond the obvious, and consider implications of its positive as well as negative meaning, in light of a Christ-centered understanding of what the Bible teaches concerning the place of possessions in our lives, we realize we are being confronted by a commandment that speaks meaningfully to some of the most vital, personal, and corporate issues of life.

To give order to our thought, we will think first about what the Seventh Commandment tells us not to do. Then we will turn to its positive meaning and, finally, will focus on a biblical understanding of the place of possessions in our lives, and on what this means for us, as individuals and as a community.

Negative Meaning

"You shall *not* steal." We are not to take things that do not belong to us or contrive to possess them by deception or fraud. This prohibition is grounded not only in obedience to God and respect for our neighbor and our neighbor's property; it is also based upon proper respect for ourselves. We children of God are to have such high regard for our neighbors and for ourselves that we do not stoop to stealing. Years ago, a person confessed that his guilt over petty thievery was increased by remembrance of this advice his father had given him when he was a little boy: "Never steal less than a million dollars because to do so is an insult to your character." That father was not suggesting that his son should try to steal more than a million, but that to go into a store and sneak a candy bar, or to cheat someone on a business deal, was beneath one's dignity. A person with proper character and conscience wouldn't do it! If everyone followed that father's advice, adjusted the amount upward to account for inflation, (in dollar value that million would be worth several million by now), and then universally follow that rule, about 99.9 percent of all stealing would be immediately eliminated.

Most of us will never be tempted to steal millions, but we are all tempted to steal lesser amounts, and often in such indirect and subtle ways that we do not realize we are stealing at all. As employees, we are tempted to steal from our employers by doing shoddy work or by being lazy on the job. As employers, we are tempted to steal from our employees by not paying a fair wage or not providing the conditions and benefits that they deserve. As students, we steal from the community by being destructive of school property, disruptive in the classroom and so careless with our work that we waste the time of the teachers who have been provided to instruct us. We can also steal by misrepresentation. "Yes," we may say, "this is a wonderful, fine-running car," and then hope that the buyer will get out of sight before the car breaks down. We can steal from the government by cheating on our taxes. A conscientious and honest decision to refuse to pay certain taxes as an act of open civil disobedience is one thing; dishonesty, scheming, and defrauding is something worse. We are especially tempted to indulge in subtle forms of stealing from large corporations. Suppose, for example, I fly to a distant city and want to inform my family I have arrived safely, but don't want to pay for the phone call. Before leaving, I tell the family that, when I arrive, I will place a person-to-person call to myself or to someone else who won't be at home. There is no charge for such a call, but I will still have conveyed my message. Although this may seem innocent, it is really stealing from the telephone company.

It is easy to rationalize these kinds of stealing. Some say they have been so often exploited and ripped-off by their employers, landlords, big companies, or by the government that, when they do these things, they are just retrieving a little of what has been stolen from them. There is certainly much legal exploitation in the world. I think it was Will Rogers who said that when a poor person steals a bucket of coal from the railroad, he goes to jail, but when a business tycoon steals the entire railroad, he goes to the top of the social register. Poor people and minority groups are often legally but immorally exploited.

There is even one majority group, namely women, who are still being robbed, through denial of equal pay for equal work. There have been and still are serious problems of entrenched institutionalized injustice that involve stealing by the rich from the poor, but none of these problems is solved by the poor stealing from the rich. There may be strange and tragic circumstances in which it is right for Robin Hood to take from the rich to save the poor, but a society of justice cannot be built by commending or condoning thievery. We can all agree it would be right to steal a would-be murderer's gun or knife and thus save someone's life, but let us again beware of transforming such bizarre exceptions into a new rule that makes it acceptable for the poor to steal from the rich, or gives one group the right to rob another. Obedience to "You shall *not* steal" is essential to our life with God, to the welfare of society, and to our own individual character.

Positive Meaning

In his explanation of the Seventh Commandment in the Small Catechism, Luther says we are to "fear and love God so that we do not take our neighbor's money or property, or get them in any dishonest way." Then he becomes positive: we are not only to refrain from stealing, we are also "to help our neighbor to improve and protect his property and means of making a living." Our greatest sins against this commandment (and most of the other commandments as well) may be in our sins of omission more than in our sins of commission. Our greatest faults are not always in what we have *done*, but in what we have *failed* to do. "Whoever knows what is right to do and fails to do it, for him it is sin." (James 4:17) This is the sin of the priest and Levite in the parable of the Good Samaritan, when they passed by on the other side. If someone had pointed a finger of blame against them, they might have replied, "Don't blame us. We didn't do anything wrong. We just kept walking!" Such statements confess some of our worst sins — sins of doing nothing, sins of failing to do the good we should have done.

We live in a world of hunger, oppression, and suffering, close at hand as well as far away. Some of these global problems are so big we can hardly comprehend them. When we think about them, we are tempted to blame other people or even to blame God for them. Jack Nelson, author of *Hunger for Justice,* tells that when he first encountered massive hunger and saw adults and children dying of malnutrition and from illnesses that could easily have been cured through minimal health care, his first feeling was to scream at God saying, "Why don't you *do* something!" But then he began to realize that in the hunger and suffering of these people, God was really screaming at *him* to do something to relieve it.

In the suffering of humanity, God is screaming at us. God is calling us to new awareness, to new commitment to alleviate this suffering, to new service of sharing and of sacrifice. The apostle Paul promises, "God is able to provide you with every blessing in abundance, so you may always have enough of everything and may provide in abundance for every good work." (2 Corinthians 9:8) The opportunity to do some of that work is as close as the offering plate we pass on Sunday morning. Agencies such as Lutheran World Relief and its Protestant, Roman Catholic, and Jewish counterparts, together with organizations such as Bread for the World and the United Way, call us to care and to share. In its positive meaning, this commandment challenges each of us to "provide in abundance for every good work." When we see our neighbors in need and fail to provide the help we are able to give, we are stealing from them just as if we had robbed bread from their hands.

The Bible and Possessions

The Seventh Commandment means (negatively) we are not to steal, and (positively) we are to share and to serve. But beyond these meanings, it also calls our basic values into question and challenges us concerning the place of possessions in our lives as persons and as a people.

The Bible has much of interest to say about possessions and property. Note these significant passages:

"Give me neither poverty nor riches; feed me with the food that is needful for me, lest I be full, and deny thee, and say, 'Who is the Lord?' or lest I be poor, and steal, and profane the name of my God." (Proverbs 30:8) This asks for *enough,* not too little, not too much. It echoes the apostle Paul: "God is able to provide you with every blessing in abundance, so that you may always have *enough* of everything . . ." (2 Corinthians 9:8; emphasis added) The Bible says, in effect, "Enough is enough." It calls us to reduce our wants to our needs.

"If you lend money to any of my people with you who is poor, you shall not be to him as a creditor and you shall not exact interest from him. If ever you take your neighbor's garment in pledge, you shall, restore it before the sun goes down . . ." (Exodus 22:25, 26) There was to be no exploitation of the poor by the rich. The basis of relationships within the family of God's people was to be compassion and not greed.

Leviticus 25 tells about the year of Jubilee. There was to be no permanent private ownership of land. Every fiftieth year all leases were to expire and all the people were to return to their ancestral estates. "The land shall not be sold in perpetuity," said the Lord, "for the land is mine . . ." (Leviticus 23:23) The earth was the Lord's, and it was not to become the permanent possession of any person. Some Christians understand these statements to prohibit private ownership of land. Tolstoy believed it was as sinful to own land as to own a slave. I am not convinced it is always wrong to own land, but I am certain some attitudes of ownership are sinful. I also believe that it is wrong for anyone to possess too much of anything and am intrigued by the idea of a graduated land tax that would parallel the progressive income tax and which would require large landowners to pay more tax per acre than those who own smaller farms. Sinful ownership fails to recognize that "the earth is the Lord's and the fullness thereof" (Psalm 24:1), and ignores the fact that we are only trustees, managers, stewards, of God's land and property.

Acts 2:44 and 4:32-35 tell about some Christians who held everything in common and of how they sold their possessions and goods and distributed them to all as any had need. It was a kind of voluntary communism expressing the basic principle "from each according to ability, to each according to need." Paul advocates similar sharing: "As a matter of equality your abundance at the present time should supply their want, so that their abundance may supply your want that there may be equality." (2 Corinthians 8:14, 15) The result was to be similar to that recorded in Exodus 16:18, "He that gathered much had nothing over, and he that gathered little had no lack."

Jesus and Possessions

Jesus didn't own anything beyond the clothes on his back. "Foxes have holes, and birds of the air have nests;" said Jesus, "but the Son of man has nowhere to lay his head." (Matthew 8:20) Clarence Jordan has described Jesus as a kind of "high-minded hobo" who had a healthy appreciation of the limited value of material things. "Take heed," Jesus said, "and beware of all covetousness for a man's life does not consist in the abundance of his possessions." (Luke 12:15) Having given that warning and stated that fact, Jesus goes on to tell the parable of the rich fool (Luke 12:16-21), and to urge his disciples to live like the birds of the air and the flowers of the field, always remembering that life is more than food and clothing. (Luke 12:22-31) We are not to be "of anxious mind" but are instead to "seek (God's) kingdom." (Luke 12:29,31) The reigning presence of God is to be our supreme treasure, not money and things thieves can steal, or fancy clothes moths can chew up and devour. (Luke 12:32-34)

In the parallel passage, in Matthew, Jesus says, "You cannot serve God and money." (Matthew 6:24) We can serve God *with* money but money is not to be a substitute for God. We are to live in the solid security of God's grace, and not just in the false security of material things.

When we take Jesus' example and teaching seriously, we discover he is challenging, not just our greed and wastefulness, but also our values and way of life. All too often we live as if life *did* consist in the abundance of our possessions. "The good life" is too often understood to consist in the luxury of much money and many things. Jesus challenges us to examine our getting and our spending, as well as our giving. Could we be so caught up in a materialistic way of life that we aren't even aware of it? Could the financial success of which we are so proud be "an abomination in the sight of God"? (Luke 16:15)

The world could not long endure another country the size of the United States consuming and wasting as we do. We are only about six percent of the world's population, but we use thirty percent of the world's energy and far more than our fair share of many of the earth's limited resources. We like to think of America as a blessing to the world, but can it be that our consuming and wasting is more of a curse than a blessing? Are we more of a problem than a solution to the world's hunger and need? Are we, in effect, robbing others of what they need in order to give ourselves what we want? Do we claim the right of luxuries for ourselves, while others do not have the basic necessities of life? Are we also stealing from our children and children's children by wasting resources now that they will need then? Jesus taught us to pray "give us (and not just me) this day our daily (not yearly) bread." (Matthew 6:11) Living out that prayer requires justice as well as charity.

Like little clouds on the horizon, times of shortage of energy and raw materials may be only the beginning of a stormy era of limitation and scarcity, not only of energy, but of many other resources, including food and water. Temporary surpluses are nothing to cheer about. They tempt us to stop conserving resources and hinder the development of alternative sources of renewable, non-polluting energy. The Old Testament tells of how Joseph saved a nation and surrounding countries from famine (see Genesis 41-45). Had Joseph related to the years of plenty as do some of our leaders to temporary abundance, all of Egypt and Jacob's family would likely have starved to death. What the world needs now is a thousand "Josephs" to challenge us all to be responsible stewards of our limited resources. If arable land, for example, is to be preserved to feed future generations, regenerative agriculture must replace practices that erode and deplete the soil.

The fact of a finite planet calls for wisdom, compassion, and courage, which the world has seldom seen.

In the needs of suffering humanity, God is crying out to us. Cries of human anguish echo the voice of Christ, who calls us to a less consumptive and more fulfilling life. If we Americans believe we need to spend nearly 1,000 million dollars a day on military self-defense, it may be that we have simply accumulated too much to defend. If this is true, we need not only reverse the arms race, but also to stop and reverse our feverish race to acquire more things we really don't need. In Christ, we are called to a new way of life consisting of trust in God and love of people — a way of life free from being possessed by possessions — a way of life that measures true riches, not in the abundance of our possessions but in the fewness of our wants.

"When we have all we need," asked E. Stanley Jones, "what more do we need?"

None of us can be certain of all the Seventh Commandment means and implies for us, but we can be sure it requires new seeing, new thinking, new caring, and new sharing. Serious study of this commandment also prompts us to reexamine all of the world's economic systems. No economic system is perfect. Like all other human institutions, all economic systems are infected with sin and folly. We wonder: how long will people continue to endure the oppression of tyrannical forms of communism? We wonder: can capitalism and free enterprise survive a prolonged period of contraction and scarcity? Are both the United States and the Soviet Union now declining empires to be superceded by dynamic new economies in other parts of the world? We should perhaps be grateful the economy of the USSR is not as competitive with our own as is that of Japan. We may also need to note the warning of a missionary who witnessed the transformation of Taiwan, in twenty years, from a primitive rural to high tech industrial society, and who predicts, that "When the Chinese industrial zones are fully developed, the United States will be in permanent recession."

Whatever may happen in that regard, what the world needs is economic systems reflective of stewardship of God's good creation and of the compassion of Christ and adequate to the challenges facing humanity. We cannot be sure what such systems will involve, but we can be confident they should not be built upon the illusion (too often common to both capitalism and communism) that life consists in the abundance of our possessions. They will value, and encourage enhancement of, the quality of human relationships far above the accumulation of great quantities of things to be consumed.

In the Sight of God?

In light of all that is stated and implied by the Seventh Commandment and the other Scriptures we have considered, how do our lives look in the sight of God who cares for each child on this planet as much as he cares for us? Are we by our careless, wasteful living stealing from the needy around us and from those who will live after us? Is the affluence, of which we are so proud, something of which we ought to be ashamed? In the cry of human need and in the voice and work of Jesus, we are called to be responsible stewards

of every good gift God has entrusted to us. We often fail to fulfill
this trust and thank God for mercy that abounds to forgive our sin.
But more than trusting forgiveness, we also ask God to enlighten,
redirect, and empower us to live with possessions in ways that more
nearly reflect the compassion and courage of Christ.

William Temple described Christianity as "the most materialistic of world religions." As God affirmed the goodness of creation
by becoming incarnate in Jesus, we affirm material "goods" as the
good gift of God and pray for the love and wisdom to use them for
the good of all God's children.

Questions and Suggestions for
Reflection and Discussion

1. Begin this discussion by listing at least a dozen ways of directly and indirectly breaking this commandment.

2. Do you agree with the advice, "Never steal less than a million dollars because to do so is an insult to your character"? What would happen if everyone were suddenly to practice that rule?

3. Is it wrong to steal from the government and wealthy corporations? Is it sinful, for example, to send messages by telephone — calling oneself collect, etc. — without paying for them? Why? Why not?

4. In what circumstances might stealing be justifiable? Do such unusual situations give anyone the right to steal when desiring to do so?

5. How do we break this commandment by sins of omission? When is "I didn't do anything" a confession of grievous sin?

6. Do you agree with Jack Nelson that God is screaming at us through the cries of the hungry and oppressed? If so, how are we to respond?

7. According to 2 Corinthians 9:8, why does God provide us with "every blessing in abundance"?

8. How much of what we possess really belongs to us? 90? 0? How much belongs to God?

9. What does Proverbs 30:8 teach us concerning the danger of both poverty and riches?

10. Who is richer — the person with abundant possessions or with few wants? What can we do to reduce our wants to our needs? When we have done that, how rich are we?

11. If the earth is the Lord's, is it sinful for individuals to own land? Why? Why not?

12. What do passages like Acts 2:44 and 4:32-35 and 2 Corinthians 8:14-15 mean for us today? Is "from each according to ability, to each according to need" a Christian principle? In what sense is there to be equality among Christians?

13. Do you agree with Clarence Jordan that Jesus was a kind of "high-minded hobo" who recognized the limited value of material things? If Jesus is our example in all things, what does this mean for us? If Jesus is correct in stating a person's life "does not

consist in the abundance of his possessions" (Luke 12:15), what changes must we make to bring our living in line with the realities of life?

14. In what does life really consist?

15. Is it possible that the personal and national wealth of which we are so proud is "an abomination in the sight of God"? (Luke 16:15) Do we have a right to luxuries for ourselves while others lack the necessities of life?

16. Of what significance is "Give us (not just me) this day our daily (not yearly) bread" (Matthew 6:11) for the fulfillment of this commandment?

17. If we had "a thousand Josephs" to guide us in responsible stewardship of the earth's resources, what do you think they would teach us to do?

18. What do the Seventh Commandment and the related biblical texts, which we have noted, teach us concerning capitalism, socialism, and communism? Is one economic system inherently more Christian than all others? Or is it true of economic systems that "none is righteous, no not one"? (Romans 3:10)

19. How does confrontation with this commandment drive us to Christ? What sins does it prompt us to confess? What then do we receive from Christ?

20. What amendment of life does this commandment challenge us to make?

21. How are we to keep, and help one another keep, this commandment?

Chapter 8

Speaking the Truth in Love

The eighth commandment focuses our attention on the use of God's gift of speech. Speech is a power for good or ill. We have all heard the old saying , "sticks and stones may break my bones, but names will never hurt me," and we know, when we reflect about it, this is not true. Names and words hurt as well as help us. Just think of all the words that have cut and wounded, or encouraged and strengthened your own life. Words are deeds and have a powerful effect upon our lives. To help direct that power and to guide our use of speech in helpful and not hurtful ways, we have been given the Eighth Commandment: "You shall not bear false witness against Your neighbor." (Exodus 20:16)

In its original context, the Eighth Commandment was understood to prohibit perjury, and stood against giving false testimony in a public hearing or court of law. That meaning still stands. But the Christian church has always understood this commandment to mean much more than that. Luther stresses this wider meaning and, in the *Small Catechism,* says this commandment means, "We are to fear and love God so that we do not betray, slander, or lie about our neighbor, but defend him, speak well of him, and explain his actions in the kindest way." In his *Large Catechism,* Luther states the teaching of this commandment concerns everyone. It means, negatively, that all talk that injures or causes offense to our neighbor is forbidden. It means, positively, that we are to speak only good of everyone, to cover the sins and infirmities of our neighbor, and to adorn our neighbors with true honor.

Ephesians 4:15 also provides a summary of the meaning of this commandment: "Speaking the truth in love, we are to grow up in every way into Him who is the head, into Christ." "Speaking the truth in love" — this is the heart of the Eighth Commandment as understood in the context of Christ. It presents two tests of all our speaking: (1) Is it true? and (2) Is it loving? Or, in other words: (1) Is it honest? and, (2) Is it kind? Truthfulness is not an adequate test of our speech. We must also ask: Is this helpful? Is it constructive? Does it build up? In this light we understand false witness against our neighbor to include unkind as well as untrue speaking in daily conversation, as well as in courtroom testimony.

Untrue and Unkind

With this dual standard in mind, we examine ourselves to see if our talking passes the test. Our most obvious failure is in speech that is neither true nor kind. All lies and deceptions which are intended to cheat, defraud, hurt, or harm someone, are clearly sinful. Such sins are so obvious it hardly seems necessary to talk about them. When we have said something which is both untrue and unkind, we have wronged our neighbor. When we are tempted to say things that are dishonest and hurtful, we know we are tempted to sin.

True but Unkind

Other situations are most perplexing. Is it ever wrong to tell the truth? In the light of our double test, the answer is clearly "Yes." It is wrong to tell the truth when it is unloving and unkind. Gossip, for example, may be true but, when it is unkind to tell something, we should not talk about it. Since we don't like people gossiping about us, we should follow the golden rule and not gossip about them. When we let the love of Christ control us, we will speak about others as we wish they would speak about us.

One of the purposes of this commandment is to protect our own and our neighbor's good name and reputation. To destroy other people's reputations is worse than destroying their property. It is worse than burning down someone's home. A house can be reubilt, but a burned reputation is sometimes impossible to restore. Luther recognized malicious gossip is a terrible and wrongful business and, therefore, teaches us not only to refrain from betraying, slandering, or lying about our neighbors, but also instructs us to defend them, speak well of them, and explain their actions in the kindest way.

It is easy to criticize and even to condemn. It is not always so easy to understand and to appreciate. J. W. Stevenson is correct when he says, "This is our human predicament; this is the confusion that we are in, that we can scarcely judge evil in others without increasing the evil in ourselves."[1] When tempted to tell hurtful truths about others, we should follow Jesus' instruction in Matthew 18:15-17. If we have a complaint about someone and want to talk about it, we are to speak to that person alone and talk face to face. If that doesn't help we are to bring along two or three witnesses and have a discussion together, and only when that fails is the problem to be shared with the Christian community. All of us have to confess that we often do exactly the opposite of Jesus' advice. We complain to everyone else first and sometimes never tell the person against whom we have a grievance. If we do not have the courage to confront that person we should maintain sacred silence and keep the complaint to ourselves.

Another example of wrongful truth-telling is what might be called spiteful honesty. It may be true that my wife wishes I were as handsome as someone she admires, but I am grateful she doesn't make a habit of telling me so. Some forms of popular psychology advocate total honesty in sharing our feelings with each other. We all long for relationships in which it is possible to be totally honest, but we must also recognize the fact that such sharing is sometimes unkind and unwise. In our book, *Be Good to Each Other: An Open Letter on Marriage,* we tell of a woman who was advised by her psychotherapist to tell her parents-in-law, with whom she and her husband were living, exactly how she sometimes felt about them. She proceeded to do so and soon discovered the problem was worse than before. Her bewildered in-laws now felt rejected and she realized they were unable to handle that kind of information; it would have been better for her to vent her feelings with her therapist and husband and to spare everyone, including herself, the suffering that resulted from such total honesty.[2]

When tempted to express truth in ways that are destructive, it is again well to remember Ephesians 4:26, "Be angry but do not sin." We are to acknowledge and appropriately express our anger, but are not to do so in ways that are sinful — in ways that are hurtful of others. In our speech, as in our actions, we are to "Be kind to one another, tenderhearted, forgiving one another as God in Christ forgave you." (Ephesians 4:32) It is especially useless, and often extremely destructive, to spend our lives complaining about what cannot be changed. We all need to regularly pray Reinhold Niebuhr's serenity prayer which has been adapted and adopted by Alcoholics Anonymous: "God, give us grace to accept with serenity the things that cannot be changed, courage to change the things that should be changed, and the wisdom to distinguish the one from the other."[3] Spiteful honesty flunks the test of kindness. Benjamin Franklin is said to have advised that before we marry we should have our eyes wide open to see what we are getting into, but after marriage we should have our eyes half shut to avoid seeing unchangeable petty things about which to complain. That good advice applies to all human relationships as well as marriage.

Another kind of false witness — "true" but hurtful — is the breaking of confidences, the sharing of secrets others have entrusted to us. An old story tells of four preachers who went fishing together. Since the fish weren't biting, one suggested that they confess their sins and weaknesses to each other. One confessed to having done a little gambling and another to occasionally having had too much to drink. The third confessed to having sneaked in to some X-rated movies. The fourth minister was reluctant to make his confession. "My sin," he said, "is much worse than anything you have confessed." But, after much encouragement, he made this confession: "I just can't keep a confidence and can hardly wait to get home and tell everyone what you have told me." That pastor's sin was worse than what the others had confessed. To betray a confidence is one of the most hurtful things we can ever do. Telling confidences is "telling the truth," but it is unkind and unloving and, therefore, sinful. Only in the most extreme exceptional circumstances, such as to save someone's life, is a pastor, or any other Christian, for that matter, justified in breaking a confidence.

Kind but Untrue

If it is wrong to tell the loveless truth, is it ever right to tell a kindly lie? Love and kindness sometimes compel us to withhold the truth. Do love and kindness sometimes compel us to shade the truth, or even to tell a lie? Before attempting an answer, we will consider several concrete situations.

I once visited a parishioner who had just been told he had terminal cancer. He made this request: "Don't tell anyone that I have cancer. My doctor assures me that I will likely have a few good

months and I don't want everyone fussing over me." The next day
another member inquired about this man's health and asked, "Does
he have cancer?" How should I answer that question? Being vowed
to secrecy, I can't say, "Yes." I certainly can't say, "He asked me
not tell anyone," because that would have told it all. Therefore, I
answered, "I don't know. They are still doing tests. It seems a puzzling kind of problem." That answer was partly true. They were going to do a few more tests, and cancer is a puzzling problem, but
strictly speaking, "I don't know" was a bold-faced lie. Months later,
after the man had died, I confessed to the inquiring member that
I had lied to him and explained the circumstances. After hearing my
story, he replied, "I think you did the right thing. In that situation,
it would have been wrong for you to tell me the truth."

As another example, recall the story of *The Hiding Place* and
of how those people hid Jews and told lies to protect them. Their
statements were kind, but untrue. Do you think they did the right
thing?

Think also of a man severely burned in an accident. His doctor
later confessed there seemed almost no chance of survival. But when
asked, "What chance do I have of recovery?" the doctor told him,
"Your chances are about fifty-fifty." That man lived, and one of
his family told me with emotion "We thank God that his doctor
lied to him. It gave him hope, without which he might have died."
This example illustrates a complex problem for medical ethics. In
The Anatomy of an Illness, Norman Cousins writes at length about
placebos — that is, medicines containing no medication, but which
are given for psychological effect.[4] They are based on deception but
they give hope and are often therapeutically effective. Is such deception justified? In one sense placebos are a lie, but they can also
be acts of love and means of healing. We may thank God when a
doctor heals through deception, but at the same time we wonder,
for the deception itself is based upon our trust in the doctor, which
can be destroyed if the deception is discovered. These are complex
and difficult questions.

Citing these examples from rare unusual circumstances is certainly not to suggest it is always right to lie. It is almost always *wrong*
to lie, but there may be unusual circumstances in which love compels us to deceive. If someone comes to your home to kill a member
of your family, you need not tell where the intended victim is hiding. With clear conscience you may boldly declare, "He left this

morning and won't be home for a week." Although literally a lie, such a statement is not a "false" witness. It is not sinful to say or do the right thing. Such a statement, which might save a life and prevent a person from committing murder, expresses responsible stewardship, both of God's good gift of life and of his good gift of speech.

Subtle Sins of Speech and Silence

Many of our worst sins of speech are not in blatant lies, but half truths and artful deception. E. Stanley Jones writes of seeing these lines from Ruskin posted on a wall in Ghandi's humble dwelling:

> The essence of lying is in deception, not in words; a lie may be told by silence, by equivocation, by accent on a syllable, by a glance of the eyes attaching a peculiar significance to a sentence; and all these kinds of lies are worse and baser by many degrees than a lie lamely worded.[5]

Such lies are altogether too common, not only in our personal conversation, but also in the standard rhetoric of politics and selling. Truth is shaded or distorted to get a vote, to make a sale, or to gain some other selfish advantage. Such deception is sin.

Another sinful habit of speech is to express our anger through complaint and criticism rather than confession. To express anger through habitual complaint and criticism is degrading to ourselves as well as to others. Thankfully, there is another way to express our negative emotions — through confession of how we feel, as a statement about ourselves rather than an attack upon another person. There is a world of difference between complaining, "You are mean and stupid," and confessing, "I feel hurt and resentful." The first creates conflict, the other invites conversation, and often prompts confession in return. Learning to share our hostility as a confession instead of a complaint may seem a little thing, but it can sometimes save a marriage and renew a family or friendship.

Another hurtful habit of speech involves the use of ridicule and "put-down" humor. Since none of us likes to be ridiculed, we should refrain from ridiculing others. "Put-down" humor is always suspect, and especially when it is at someone else's expense. If we wish to laugh at someone, we do well to learn to laugh at ourselves, and especially when tempted to take ourselves too seriously. It requires no more effort to be habitually appreciative and encouraging than to be cynical and sarcastic.

We also sin against this commandment by keeping silent when we ought to speak. "Speaking the truth in love" requires us to speak up for those who are being maligned or unfairly criticized. To keep silent when we should speak well of someone is a serious sin of omission. Such speaking often requires courage as well as kindness. Once again, the golden rule applies — as we are grateful when others speak up for us, we should be bold in speaking up for them.

Speech that Builds Up

As we seek to avoid hurtful speech and sinful silence, we also seek ways of speaking which are helpful and constructive — which build up rather than tear down. One way of doing so is to confess our gratitude as well as our grievances. We need not be like the silent husband who once confided to his friend, "I love my wife so much that I almost told her so." When asked, by his wife, "Do you still love me?" one such husband is reported to have replied, "I told you that I loved you when we got married and if I change my mind I'll let you know." We don't live well on last week's cold potatoes, nor do we live well on such cold conversation. We need continued reassurance of the warmth of honest love. The truth of love, kindly and openly shared, renews our lives and our relationships.

One way of showing appreciation is through "I like it when . . ." comments. In *Be Good To Each Other* we urge married couples to do a little exercise in which they complete the statement, "I like it when . . ." in several different ways and then share their appreciation with each other in comments such as, "I like it when you tell me what you are feeling" or "I like it when you fix the carrots that way."[6] Sharing appreciation can become the honest habit of our common conversation in family, friendship, and business, as well as in marriage. Such sharing of gratitude can transform our conversation into a means of grace which gives encouragement and joy.

"Speaking the truth in love" can also mean strong confrontation with a person who has an alcohol problem, or who is living in some other way which is destructive of self and others. Truthful love means telling a reluctant child, "You are ill and must see a doctor." It can also mean telling a hostile adult, "I believe that you have an unhealthy dependence on alcohol and that you should seek treatment." Such confrontation may seem cruel, but it is much kinder, as well as more honest, than the fearful and sometimes spiteful "enabling" that often helps to perpetuate the problem. To those who reject us for it, we can inquire, as did the apostle Paul, "Have I then become your enemy by telling you the truth?" (Galatians 4:16)

Forgiven and Being Healed

By speech and silence, by words spoken and by others left unsaid, we have sinned against this commandment and against people we are to love. We turn again to God's promises in Christ, asking forgiveness and trusting God's mercy. We thank God for still loving us in spite of our misuse of his gift of speech.

Beyond trusting forgiveness, we pray to learn better habits of speaking — better ways of sharing truth with love. Someone has suggested when we open our mouths, we let people look into our hearts and minds. Jesus said the same: "For out of the abundance of the heart, the mouth speaks." (Matthew 12:34) "Speaking the truth with love" requires change of heart as well as habits. As we ponder God's gift of speech we also thank God that the Holy Spirit is at work within us to produce those "fruit of the Spirit" qualities, beginning with "love" and going on to "patience, kindness, goodness" and ending with "gentleness" and "self-control." (Gal. 5:22) We need those qualities to enable our proper speaking as well as proper living. We pray to be healed from the inside out and so enabled to live with integrity and compassion that we will be honest and kind, truthful and loving, in all our speaking.

ENDNOTES

[1] J. W. Stevenson, *God in My Unbelief.* New York: Harper & Row, 1963, p. 54.

[2] Lowell and Carol Erdahl, *Be Good to Each Other,* p. 19.

[3] Reinhold Niebuhr, *Justice and Mercy,* edited by Ursula Niebuhr. New York: Harper & Row, 1974, Epigraph following title page.

[4] Norman Cousins, *Anatomy of an Illness.* New York: W. W. Norton, 1979.

[5] E. Stanley Jones, *Mahatma Ghandi, An Interpretation.* New York: Abingdon-Cokesbury, 1948, p. 123.

[6] Lowell and Carol Erdahl, *Be Good to Each Other,* p. 13.

Questions and Suggestions for
Reflection and Discussion

1. Do you agree that "words are deeds"? Share examples of how words have wounded or encouraged you.

2. Why are we justified in understanding the Eighth Commandment to relate not only to perjury, but to total stewardship of the gift of speech?

3. Can any group operate with total dishonesty? Don't even a band of thieves need to be able to trust each other? What does this tell us about how this commandment, like all the commandments, is written in the nature of human relationships and not only in the text of the Bible?

4. Does all Christian speech need to pass the test of both truth and love? Why? Are there additional tests? Might the question, "Is it necessary"? be another?

5. List and discuss examples of situations in which it is wrong to tell the truth.

6. Study Matthew 18:15-17 and give examples of how we fail to put it in practice and when we should do so.

7. In what circumstances is it better to discuss a problem with a counselor than with the person with whom we are experiencing the difficulty?

8. Are there any circumstances in which it is right for a pastor or a counselor to break a confidence? If so, when?

9. List and discuss situations in which you believe it would be right to tell a lie. Do such exceptions justify the practices of established deception? Why? Why not?

10. What is the difference between telling a lie in an exceptional circumstance and becoming an habitual liar or accepting deception as standard procedure?

11. Discuss the difference between sharing negative feelings as a confession of one's own experience rather than as a criticism of another person. What is the difference between saying, "I feel hurt," and saying, "You are hateful"? Or even between, "I didn't make myself clear," and "You don't understand"?

12. How does the Eighth Commandment relate to our use of sarcasm, ridicule and "put-down" humor?

13. List and discuss situations in which it would be sinful to keep silent. When would it be wrong to speak up?

14. We keep this commandment by building up rather than tearing down. How do we verbally build each other up? Invite members of the group to share "I like it when . . ." comments with each other, to illustrate ways of doing so.

15. Note and discuss situations in which it is sometimes necessary to confront a person with unpleasant truth. Are we sometimes to risk becoming someone's enemy by telling the truth? When required to tell such truth, how should we go about it?

16. How does this commandment drive us to Christ? What sins does it prompt us to confess? What then do we receive from Christ?

17. What amendment of life does this commandment challenge us to make?

18. How do we keep, and help each other keep, this commandment?

Chapter 9

Out of the Heart

In our reflections on the Ten Commandments we have noted their connection to almost every area of our personal and public life. The first three commandments deal with our relationship with God; the other seven with our relationships with people. Each of these seven touches upon a specific aspect of life. The fourth commandment deals with our relationships with parents and others in authority, the fifth with reverence for life, the sixth with our sexuality, the seventh with our use of money and things, the eighth with our stewardship of the gift of speech.

In our concluding thoughts on the eighth commandment, we noted how Jesus saw a concrete connection between the words of our mouths and the attitudes of our hearts: "Out of the abundance of the heart, the mouth speaks." (Matthew 12:34) Now, as we focus on the ninth and tenth commandments, we see that all sin and goodness are matters of the heart. "For out of the heart," said Jesus, "come evil thoughts, murder, adultery, fornication, theft, false witness, slander." (Matthew 15:19) (Note how many items in this list relate directly to the commandments we have considered.) Jesus indicates good deeds are also matters of the heart. "For no good tree bears bad fruit, nor again does a bad tree bear good fruit; for each tree is known by its own fruit . . . The good man out of the good treasure of his heart produces good, the evil man out of his evil treasure produces evil; for out of the abundance of the heart his mouth speaks." (Luke 6:43-45)

The story is told of how Abraham Lincoln and a rushing pedestrian once collided at the corner of a Washington building. As they picked themselves up, Lincoln was accosted by curses for not looking where he was going, to which he is said to have replied, "My friend, there is something wrong with you on the inside." Like the teaching of Jesus, that story reminds us that immorality is not just a matter of outward actions, but of something being *wrong* with us on the inside. Morality springs from that which is *right* on the inside.

The teaching of Jesus and the Lincoln story lead us into consideration of the meaning of the ninth and tenth commandments, which deal specifically with matters of the heart. As noted earlier, these are really one commandment and are numbered as one by both the Hebrew community and most Protestants. The Roman Catholic-Lutheran numbering is based upon a division of Exodus 20:17. Had it been based upon the parallel passage in Deuteronomy 5:21, there would be a different order because, in that passage, "wife" comes before "house," and may mean "household," referring to everything listed separately. The message of Exodus and Deuteronomy is, however, essentially the same and is summed up in the new translation of Luther's Small Catechism: "You shall not covet your neighbor's house. You shall not covet your neighbor's wife, or his manservant, or his maidservant, or his cattle, or anything that is your neighbor's."

What Is It to Covet?

"You shall not covet." What does this commandment forbid? What does Jesus warn us against when he says, "Take heed, and beware of all covetousness; for a man's life does not consist in the abundance of his possessions"? (Luke 12:15) To covet is to desire, but all desiring is not covetous. As Christians we do not believe, as do some followers of Eastern religions, that desire itself is the source of all evil. We believe that many desires are good, healthy, and normal. They are a sign of life. God has built them into us. At the same time, we know some desires are sinful, so we have the problem of separating right from wrong desire. In the light of Christ, it seems safe to say it is right for us to desire everything God wants for us — everything good for us — everything we need and can receive without harming someone else. On the other hand, it is, therefore, wrong to desire things hurtful for us, things we should not have, or things which are more needful to someone else. What is prohibited in the ninth and tenth commandments is not wholesome yearning for fullness of life, but greedy, envious, self-indulgent self-seeking.

94

In our consideration of adultery, we made a distinction between loving and lusting. Covetousness is a kind of lusting, not only for sex, but for anything and everything we greedily seek to possess. The image of the miser fondling his money is one picture of that kind of lustful covetousness. The greedy politician lusting after power is another. Paul Tournier says, "The secret sin, less visible than overt wrongdoing is covetousness. Now, covetousness is another way of saying thirst for power." This sin, says Tournier, is "the underlying source of all conflicts."[1]

Coveting People

It is often said we are to love people and to use things; we get into trouble when we start loving things and using people. Our reflections on these commandments will focus on the love and misuse of things, but we must also note they specifically reject the lustful desiring of people: "You shall not covet your neighbor's wife or his manservant or his maidservant." (Exodus 20:17) From our greedy perspective, it often seems "the grass is greener on the other side of the fence." We are often more envious of our neighbor's people than our neighbor's grass. We can be somewhat objective about the grass, but we are prone to fantasize about the people: the neighbor's wife seems so beautiful and vivacious, the neighbor's husband so kind and caring. We see our own partners at their worst, and fantasize the neighbor's spouse to be far better than her or his best. Similarly, we know our employees' shortcomings and imagine the neighboring employer's workers to be flawless. Lured by covetous lust for such idealized people, many have acted in ways that resulted in misery for everyone involved.

But, what if it is really true — the neighbor's spouse is more beautiful, more handsome, more intelligent, more loving than our own, and the competitor's employees are more industrious than ours? Are we then justified in greedily desiring to have them and in attempting to entice them away to become our own? These commandments say, "No!" In his explanation, Luther again underscores the positive meaning of these commandments and stresses we are to encourage our neighbor's spouse and employees to remain faithful in their present relationships. If we truly care for our neighbors we will rejoice in their good fortune, even in their having spouses more attractive than our own, and instead of tempting them to leave, we will encourage their continued loyalty. If this seems too much to ask, remember it is nothing more than Jesus requires in the Golden Rule. This aspect of the meaning of the Ninth and Tenth commandments asks only that we treat our neighbors in exactly the same way we wish them to treat us. In a free market economy, this need not be understood legalistically to prohibit all movement of employees from one firm to another, but it does express a clear word of judgment concerning the greedy pursuit (and often literal buying and selling) of human beings, whether for a more productive company, a more winning team, or a more perfect spouse.

Coveting Things

When we start loving *things* — when our cars become love objects and not just means of transportation; when life begins to consist in the abundance of our possessions — when our chief preoccupation is to acquire more and more; when we begin to caress and fondle our possessions in our minds, if not with our hands; then we are in big trouble because we are living a distorted, sinful, covetous life.

What is revealed when we look at ourselves in the mirror of the Ninth and Tenth commandments? Do we see a person desiring only what we really need? Only things that are good for us? Only things we can possess without harm to others? Or do we see a graspy, greedy, envious, jealous person lusting covetously to satisfy pride and self-indulgence? Do we want some things only because others have them, or even only to have more than they do?

We need to look long and hard at ourselves in the mirror of these commandments, but even that may not be enough. We may need to have someone who isn't caught up in our affluent way of life — someone from another culture and continent — point out our sin against these commandments. Each of us has a visual blind spot. Put two dots about three inches apart on a piece of paper. Close your right eye and focus your left eye on the right dot; then move the paper back and forth until the left dot disappears. It is there on the paper, but you can't see it. We have similar kinds of spiritual blind spots, especially in terms of seeing our own sins. We can be so caught up in our consuming we are unaware of our coveting.

A friend once told of visiting with an African pastor who had traveled in the United States. They discussed certain African marriage customs, including polygamy, that still exist in some Christian communities. My friend expressed surprise that Christians could still follow such customs. The African pastor then confessed he was equally surprised that American Christians could be so greedily possessive and so often wasteful of wealth and property. He wondered how we could be so preoccupied with all these material things and still call ourselves Christians.

There would be a great scandal in any of our congregations if it were discovered a member had two wives or two husbands. But we don't think it a scandal to have two cars or two houses or two bank accounts or twice or even three or ten times as much as we need of everything. Such affluence seems natural to us. It's just our way of life. And yet is it possible that the greedy, acquisitive covetousness that has led to the accumulation of all these things is a sin more evil in the sight of God than an African convert's keeping his two wives? It seems almost unpatriotic and un-American to ask such a question. We celebrate the great American success story and take our way of life for granted. But, when we look in the mirror of these commandments and listen to Jesus' words, "Take heed, and beware of all covetousness; for a man's life does not consist in the abundance of his possessions" (Luke 12:15), we must wonder if our prosperity is a witness to God's glory or to our greed.

Are We Following Jesus?

In *The Politics of Jesus,* John Howard Yoder suggests there are two aspects of Jesus' life and teaching most Christians do not follow. One of these is Jesus' teaching and example concerning violence, killing, and war. The other is Jesus' teaching and example concerning a proper attitude toward, and use of, possessions, property, money, and things. Jesus lived simply. He taught his disciples, and teaches us, "Do not lay up for yourselves treasures on earth, where moth and rust consume and where thieves break in and steal." (Matthew 6:19) Jesus' statement that a person's life "does not consist in the abundance of his possessions" is a fact of life. It is not true just because Jesus said it; Jesus said it because it is true, and when sickness strikes us or a loved one, we know it to be true. Everything Jesus said and did underscores the fact that life does not consist in money and things, but in trusting the love of God, and in living with love toward one another.

We confess to believe Jesus but are often so caught up in conformity to our culture that our attitudes and actions are little different from those of non-Christians, nearby and around the world. In fact, people who do follow Jesus' attitudes toward violence and possessions often seem strange to us. I recall meeting one of those "strange" people. She was an older woman called "Peace Pilgrim," who had resolved years ago that until others had the basic necessities of life, she would reduce her wants to her basic needs. She seemed strange, but when she spoke, we heard an amazingly free, radiant, and joyful person. She did not suggest we live exactly as she did, but it was apparent she had learned something that Jesus is trying to teach us all. She told, for example, of visiting a woman who was extremely burdened with the care of her large home. When Peace Pilgrim suggested she might get a smaller place the lady replied, "I can't do that because I have to have room for all my furniture." Are we living to provide for our furniture? Does life consist in the abundance of our furniture or whatever else our prize possessions happen to be? Do we possess our possessions as gifts of God to be used in his service, or are we possessed by our possessions so that we are serving them instead of using them to serve others?

How do we get free from irrational and often idolatrous preoccupation with money, goods, possessions, and things? Paul says we are to "put to death . . . covetousness which is idolatry." (Colossians 3:5) But how do we do it? How can we be set free from captivity to a covetous culture and a greedy heart?

A Double Corrective

We need healing both of head and of heart. Our thinking needs to be corrected so that we realize that more is not always better and that small can be beautiful. This is not to romanticize poverty. Poverty can be oppressive and destructive of both dignity and opportunity. Most of us, however, are struggling more with the problems of prosperity than of poverty. We Americans with average, or even below average, incomes are still among the richest people in the world. We need to learn that living with less can mean better living. The "good life" means quality and not just quantity. John Ruskin spoke of this fact when he said:

*THERE IS NO WEALTH BUT LIFE. Life, including all its powers
of love, of joy, and of admiration. That country is richest which
nourishes the greatest number of noble and happy human beings;
that man is richest who, having perfected the functions of his own
life to the utmost, has also the widest helpful influence, both personal, and by means of his possessions, over the lives of others.''*[2]

A truly high standard of living is not measured in numbers of cars
and color TV sets, but in the qualities of faith, hope and love taught
by Jesus.

As we sense the limits of a finite planet and realize the dream
of endless expansion and growth is an illusion, it is as if the very
stones are crying out and saying, "Listen to Jesus, limit your crav-
ing and your consuming, seek fullness of life in an adventure of being loved and in loving."

Corrected thinking is a necessary but insufficient cure of covetousness. We require healing of our hearts as well as of our heads.
We need to have "our hearts fixed" as one of the old prayers puts
it, "where true joys are to be found." We need transformation as
well as education — to be converted, to be born over and over again
into new life, lived by the goodness and grace of God, and in caring
and sharing with people. We need to be set free from the faithless
fear and foolish pride that tempt us to greedy and graspy living. Facing the commandments on coveting, in the context of Christ, calls
us to repentance — to turn again, in trust and surrender, to the forgiving and healing Spirit of God. When grace grasps us, we begin
to be so busy thanking God for his blessings and sharing with others,
that we don't have time to be covetously preoccupied with getting
more for ourselves. We begin to learn the secret of true riches. Some
try to become rich by acquiring all they want. They are like the fa-
mous farmer who said, "I'm not greedy, I just want the land next
to mine." Needless to say, that farmer would never be satisfied until he owned the entire continent! Thank God there is another way
to be rich, namely by reducing our wants to our needs — to be rich
not in the abundance of our possessions, but in the fewness of our
wants. The apostle Paul promises, "God is able to provide you with
every blessing in abundance, so that you may always have enough
of everything." (2 Corinthians 9:8) Note Paul says "enough," which
is neither too much nor too little. First Timothy 6:6-8 teaches, "There
is great gain in godliness with contentment; for we have brought
nothing into the world, and we cannot take anything out of the

world; but if we have food and clothing, with these we shall be content." Therefore, we do well to pray using these ancient words of widsom: "Give me neither poverty nor riches; feed me with the food that is needful for me, lest I be full and deny thee, and say, 'Who Is the Lord?' or lest I be poor' and steal, and profane the name of my God." (Proverbs 30:8-9)

Having received "the unsearchable riches of Christ" (Ephesians 3:8), we are being transformed from greed to gratitude and from grasping to giving. When rejoicing in the love of God and forgetting ourselves in service of others, we have fixed our hearts "where true joys are to be found." In that joy, covetousness is consumed by gratitude and self-seeking by self-giving.

ENDNOTES

[1]Paul Tournier, *The Violence Within,* New YOrk: Harper and Row, 1978, p. 118.

[2]John Ruskin, *Unto This Last,* Essay IV Quoted by Kenneth Clark, Editor, *Ruskin Today.* New York: Holt, Rinehart and Winston, 1964, pp. 273-74.

Questions and Suggestions for
Reflection and Discussion

1.What does Jesus mean when he speaks of the good and evil treasure of a person's heart? What is the difference between people who are right or wrong on the inside? Is anyone purely one or the other?

2. Do you agree we are to love people and use things, and that we get into trouble when we love things and use people? What happens when we make this mistake?

3. How should we deal with temptations to covet people that are based on idealized fantasies?

4. How should we deal with such temptations when they are based on the fact that another person's spouse or employee is objectively more desirable than our own?

5. To what extent do we have moral blind spots that keep us from seeing our covetousness? How can we help each other in this regard?

6. What is the difference between healthy/holy admiration and desires and sick/sinful greed and covetousness?

7. List and discuss ways in which it is right for us to desire things for ourselves.

8. List and discuss ways in which it is wrong for us to desire things for ourselves.

9. Compare the distinction between loving and lusting with that between desiring and coveting.

10. To what extent has covetousness become an accepted sin, and even pseudo virtue, in our society?

11. According to Luke 12:15, upon what fact of life is Jesus' warning against covetousness based? Do most Americans acknowledge this fact?

12. How might we be considered strange if we were to really live by this teaching of Jesus?

13. Paul describes "covetousness" as "idolatry." (Colossians 3:5) Discuss how idolatry is involved in the breaking of each of commandments four through ten.

14. Do you agree we need a double corrective of head and heart in order to be cured of covetousness? What might this involve? By

what power is it possible?

15. How does confrontation with these commandments drive us to Christ? What sins do they prompt us to confess? What then do we receive from Christ?

16. What amendment of life do these commandments challenge us to make?

17. How can we keep, and help one another keep, these commandments?

Chapter 10

Love: The First and Final Word

As Christians, we understand the Old Testament in light of the New and everything in the Bible, including the Ten Commandments, in light of Jesus Christ. Having looked at them individually, we now turn to selected statements from Jesus and the apostle Paul, which sum up the Ten Commandments and set them clearly in the context of Christ.

Love is Central

A lawyer asks Jesus, "Teacher, which is the great commandment in the law?" Jesus answers by quoting Deuteronomy 6:4 and Leviticus 19:18: "You shall love the Lord your God with all your heart, and with all your soul, and with all your mind. This is the great and first commandment. And a second is like it, You shall love your neighbor as yourself. On these two commandments depend all the law and the prophets." (Matthew 22:36-40)

The apostle Paul gives a similar summary: "Owe no one anything, except to love one another; for he who loves his neighbor has fulfilled the law. The commandments, 'You shall not commit adultery, You shall not kill, You shall not steal, You shall not covet,' and 'any other commandment,' are summed up in this sentence, 'You shall love your neighbor as yourself.' Love does no wrong to a neighbor; therefore love is the fulfilling of the law." (Romans 13:8-10) Paul also says, "For you were called to freedom . . . only do not use your freedom as an opportunity for the flesh, but through love be servants of one another. For the whole law is fulfilled in one word, 'You shall love your neighbor as yourself'." (Galatians 5:13-14)

We also recall these words of Jesus: "I have given you an

example that you also should do as I have done to you . . . A new commandment I give to you, that you love one another; even as I have loved you, that you also love one another. By this all . . . will know that you are my disciples, if you have love for one another" (John 13:15, 34, 35), and again, "this is my commandment, that you love one another as I have loved you." (John 15:12)

In Christ, the first and final word is *love:* "For God so loved the world that he gave his only Son, that whoever believes in him should not perish but have eternal life." (John 3:16) "Love never ends . . . faith, hope, love abide, these three: but the greatest of these is love." (1 Corinthians 13:8 and 13) "We love, because God first loved us." (1 John 4:19)

Ten Gifts of Love

As stressed earlier, the Ten Commandments are God's gift of love to a delivered people. The first word in both Old Testament accounts of the Ten Commandments proclaims, "I am the Lord your God, who brought you out of the land of Egypt, out of the house of bondage." (Exodus 20:2 and Deuteronomy 5:6) It does not say, "If you keep these commandments, then I will set you free." It says rather, "I *have* set you free! You *are* my delivered people!" Then there is an implied "therefore" — "*Therefore,* have no other gods before me. *Therefore,* reverence my name. *Therefore,* remember the sabbath day, to keep it holy. *Therefore,* honor your parents and people in authority. *Therefore,* do not kill, do not commit adultery, do not steal, do not bear false witness, do not covet."

These commandments are not a legalistic ladder by which we climb to God. They are gifts from a God of love, given to guide us in our living and to convict and correct us when we fail to live with love. In the context of the love we know in Christ, Jesus' first commandment to love God is heard, not as a heavy obligation ordering us to feel kindly toward the divine, but as a gracious invitation to let God love us and forgive us, to let God be God for us in mercy and power. We love God when in trust, surrender, and yielding we depend upon God's love and obey God's will. Then, in Jesus' second commandment to love our neighbor, Jesus invites us to give ourselves away in compassionate caring and sharing with one another.

Our proper response to the Ten Commandments and to their summaries, in the words of Jesus and Paul, is not just to make a resolution saying, "I'm going to try hard to keep all these command-ments," but rather, to be called out of ourselves into a new adven-ture of being loved and lifted by the mercy and power of God, and then being loved into loving others. At its center, the Christian life is letting go of ourselves in trust toward God, and letting go of our-selves in love and caring toward people.

Christ's word of grace assures us daily that we, like those who first received the Ten Commandments, are a delivered people. We haven't been delivered out of literal bondage and slavery in Egypt, but we have been delivered from bondage to sin and death, and brought into the new life and liberty of the children of God. In Christ, we are set free from slavery to self-preoccupation, self-centeredness and self-seeking. Christ loves and lures us day by day, and moment by moment, into a new life of abandonment, in which we rest in the love of God and work to serve our neighbors.

Enabled and Obedient

It is significant, as well as interesting, that the New Testament speaks of our love as both the work of the Holy Spirit and as our obedient response to the command of God and the need of our neigh-bor. In Galatians 5:22 the first "fruit of the Spirit" is "love." Love is the result of the transforming, healing presence of God within us. In Christ, we are being loved into loving. We all need to be healed of hatreds, jealousies, lusts, resentments, and indifference that in-fect our lives. Such healing is not the result of self-centered striving; it is the gracious work of the Spirit of God.

But even as we are being healed by the Spirit of God, we are also commanded to love. The parable of the Good Samaritan follows a lawyer's summary of the law, in terms of love of God and love of neighbor. When Jesus commends his statement, the lawyer asks, "And who is my neighbor?" Then follows the story of the priest and Levite who "passed by on the other side" and of the Good Samaritan who helped the person in need. At the end of the story Jesus says to the lawyer and to us "Go and do likewise." (Luke 10:37) This is a concrete expression of Jesus' commandment to love. If Jesus commands it, we must be able to do it.

We cannot, by self-effort, create in ourselves an attitude of com-passion toward another person. That is the work of the Holy Spirit. But we can choose to act with compassion — to help and to share.

This kind of love is not a matter of liking someone. We are certainly invited to love the people we like, and there are many ways of doing that, but we are also commanded to love people we *don't* like. Jesus specifically commands us to "Love your enemies," and spells out the meaning of that love, not in warm feeling but in concrete action: "Do good to those who hate you, bless those who curse you, pray for those who abuse you." (Luke 6:27-28) The apostle Paul says, "As we have opportunity, let us do good to all . . . and especially to those who are of the household of faith." (Galatians 6:10) We can't like everyone, but we *can* follow John Brantner's suggestion to "look at people and wish them well." We can't like everyone but we can seek to do good to everyone.

Suppose we dislike someone who has done us harm. Then imagine that we come upon a car accident in which that person has been seriously injured. What do we do in that situation? If we are obedient to Christ, we act with love. That doesn't mean having a sudden awakening of affection for that person, but it does mean stopping to help. We call an ambulance, put on a tourniquet, and do whatever else we can to help the injured "enemy." To provide such help is to act with love and that is what we are commanded and can choose to do.

Love of enemies relates to global as well as personal issues. Nikita Khrushchev once said that, while he liked a lot in the Bible, he did not agree with Jesus' teachings about loving our enemies and turning the other cheek. "If someone strikes me on one cheek," he said, "I will knock his block off." Hearing that, most of us need to confess that we are often better followers of Khrushchev than of Christ. When we are wronged or threatened, we often respond with fear, contempt, and hatred. We strike out with vengeance and retaliation. To advocate loving our international enemies strikes some Christians as naive and unrealistic. Yet, when we realize that the way violence has brought civilization, and perhaps all humanity, to the brink of extinction, we wonder who is more naive — Jesus or those who continually call for more bombs and more vengeance? Jesus is not a sentimental dreamer. Jesus is the world's greatest realist. "Love or perish" is now the choice before us. One concrete expression of such realistic love would be for us to begin to care for the Soviet Union's sense of security as well as for our own. Increasing their insecurity makes us both less secure. Decreasing their fears of us makes us both more secure.

Someone has suggested the leaders of both the USA and USSR should agree they would not push the nuclear button until each had personally killed fifty of the "enemy's" children. If they retained any semblance of either Christianity or humanity, no leaders of any nation would then ever push the button. Our revulsion against such a barbaric act witnesses to the far greater barbarism and lovelessness of building and willing to use doomsday weapons that can destroy God's children by the millions. If it were true of all Christians that "the love of Christ controls us" (2 Corinthians 5:14), our love of those we call our enemies would compel us to work for the abolition of the institutions of war and war-making, and for the creation of new structures of international reconciliation and global security, that make for greater justice, freedom, and peace on earth.

Love Fulfills the Law

All of the commandments, says Paul, are summed up in the command to love. "Love does no wrong to a neighbor; therefore love is the fulfilling of the law." (Romans 13:10) Sin is not just acting against rules in a book. Sin is acting against life. Sin is worse than bad; it is bad for us and bad for everybody. Sin is hurtful. Sin is sand in the gears of life. Love, on the other hand, is helpful. Put positively, Paul says, "Love is that which does good to our neighbors." Sin tears down. Love builds up. Sin destroys life. Love creates, enables, and ennobles life. Love, like God who is love, is always on the side of life.

The world's best picture of such love is in the life of Jesus. On the night before he was crucified, John tells us, Jesus took a bowl, washed his disciple's feet, and said, "Do you know what I have done to you? . . . I have given you an example, that you also should do as I have done to you." (John 13:12 and 15) And then, a few verses later in the same setting, Jesus says,,"A new commandment I give to you that you love one another; even as I have loved you." (John 13:34) Here is a standard higher than the Golden Rule. The Golden Rule is good. Jesus teaches it: "Whatever you wish that others would do to you, do so to them." (Matthew 7:12) But here is a higher rule — we might call it "the diamond rule" — that says in effect: "Do unto others *as I have done* unto you." Here the standard is not self but Jesus, not self-interest but Christ-likeness, and that is the highest standard the world has ever seen. At the summit of that standard, stands a cross. Having said again, "Love one another as I have loved you" (John 15:12), Jesus goes on to say "Greater love has no man than this, that a man lay down his life for his friends." (John 15:13)

Jesus makes his command, to love others as he loves us, specific in the great commissions: "As the Father has sent me even so I send you" (John 20:21); "Go therefore and make disciples of all nations . . ." (Matthew 28:19); "You shall receive power when the Holy Spirit has come upon you and you shall be my witnesses . . . to the end of the earth." (Acts 1:8) Love is expressed in personal caring for those near us, in our gifts of money (which Harry Emerson Fosdick called "our time and talent in portable form"), given for the cause of Christ, in work for freedom, peace, and justice (which Joseph Sittler describes as "love operating at a distance") and in witnessing by the power of the Holy Spirit that all the world may know the Gospel of God's saving grace in Christ.

In His Steps

It is awesome to be called to follow the Christ of the cross in Jesus' way of love! To take Jesus as our example, to seek to live in imitation of Christ, to "follow in his steps" (1 Peter 2:21), is a difficult and dangerous business. John Howard Yoder suggests following Jesus means loving in situations where it is unpopular and costly to love. Bearing the cross of Christ is not just enduring the pain and trouble of earthly life. Everyone has to do that. Jesus' cross witnesses to the cost of Christ-like living in a world where love gets crucified. The cross reveals the cost of Christ-like nonconformity in a sinful world. Jesus was not crucified for being a cheerleader for the religious and political people in power. He was crucified because he challenged the self-righteous, as well as the self-indulgent— because he chose the way of service and love, rather than support the prevailing powers in their contempt for people. To follow Jesus in the way of love still means to act with Christ-like nonconformity. Such action is no more popular now than it was then. I doubt there has ever been a generation in which Jesus would not have been rejected by the people in power. Does our lack of experience, of the kind of suffering symbolized by the cross, witness to the unique Christ-likeness of our generation or to our being more "conformed to this world" (Romans 12:2) than controlled by "the love of Christ"? (2 Corinthians 5:14)

The First and Final Word

Love is the first and final word. We are created by the love of God, for the love of people. Among all our human abilities — intelligence, imagination, intuition, physical strength, and agility — none is more significant than our capacity to receive and to give love. We may lack the intelligence to be first in our class. We may lack the imagination and intuition to become great poets or novelists. We may lack the physical strength and agility to become star athletes. But, whatever we lack, we have a God-given capacity to be loved and to grow in love toward others.

In Christ, God loves us now and will love us forever. We may feel forsaken and forgotten, but there are people who love and want to care for us. There are also many who need our love and care. We are created, redeemed, and commissioned to be people of love. The healing, Holy Spirit of God works now to make love more and more abound within and through us. By that power, Christ sends us to live in the compassion of God and with compassion toward others. Living in Christ, we begin not only to keep the Ten Commandments and fulfill God's purpose for our lives, but also to be true to ourselves by fulfilling our deepest and highest yearning — to be loved and to give ourselves in loving.

Questions and Suggestions for
Reflection and Discussion

1. Do you agree that, as Christians, we understand the Old Testament in light of the New, and everything in the Bible in the light of Jesus Christ? In what sense is Jesus, who is Lord of all, also Lord of the Bible?

2. How do Jesus' "two commandments" on which "depend all the law and the prophets" relate to the main divisions (1-3 and 4-7) of the Ten Commandments following the Lutheran/Roman Catholic numbering system?

3. In what ways is Jesus' summary of the law in Matthew 22:36-40 more comprehensive than that of Paul in Romans 13:8-10 and Galatians 5:13-14? What does Paul omit? Does Paul really sum up "the whole law" or only that which relates to our dealings with people but not with God?

4. What is "new" about Jesus' "new commandment"? Discuss the significance of this newness.

5. Do you agree there is an implied "therefore" between Exodus 20:2 and Deuteronomy 5:6, and each of the commandments that follow? What is the point of this observation?

6. In what sense is the command to love God also a gracious invitation to let God love and forgive us? Is there even a sense in which Jesus changes this commandment from an obligation of law to an invitation of the Gospel? Explain your answer.

7. What does the statement, "At its center the Christian life is letting go of ourselves in trust toward God and letting go of ourselves in love and caring toward people" mean to you? What is involved in "letting go" toward God? Toward people?

8. What is meant by "a new life of abandonment"? In what sense are we, as Christians, to be simultaneously at rest and at work? How does an ocean liner or a swimmer illustrate such simultaneous resting and working?

9. Discuss how our love is both "the fruit of the Spirit" and action in obedience to the command of Christ. How do these two go together?

10. What is the difference between loving and liking? How can we love people we don't like?

11. How do we love our enemies? What does this imply concerning policies of instant retaliation and a massive assured destruction?

12. What do we say to those who accuse Jesus of being naive for recommending love of the enemy? Are those who fight evil with Jesus' weapons more naive than those who fight with the devil's weapons? Is Jesus an idealist or a realist?

13. Discuss ways in which "sin is sand in the gears of life." How is sin not just bad, but bad for us and everybody? What does this suggest concerning our understanding of sin?

14. If sin degrades and destroys life, what gives and ennobles life? What is the source of this power and this life?

15. Compare "the Golden Rule" with "the diamond rule." Since Jesus affirms both, how do they relate to each other and to our daily living?

16. Discuss the moral principle "so act that everyone could do as you are doing." Ask of every contemplated action, "Would it be well if everyone acted this way?" How might this principle help us make wiser choices?

17. How does the cross of Jesus reveal the cost of Christ-like nonconformity in a sinful world? What does this mean for us? Are we sometimes "crucified" for being more like the thieves than like Jesus? What would likely happen to us if we were to really live fully controlled by the love of Christ?

18. Do you agree our most significant human abilities are the capacity to receive and give love? Why? Why not? What makes it possible for us to exercise these capacities?

19. How does confrontation with New Testament interpretations of the Ten Commandments drive us to Christ? What sins do they prompt us to confess? What then do we receive from Christ?

20. What amendments of life do these teachings prompt us to make?

21. How can we keep, and help one another keep, the commandments of Christ?